ETERNITY

Heaven or Hell?

ETERNITY
Heaven or Hell?

"He who believes in the Son has eternal life; but he who does not believe the Son shall not see life, but the wrath of God abides on him"
— John 3:36 (NASV)

"Life offers many choices. Eternity offers only two." — Author Unknown

Dr. David R. Reagan

LAMB & LION MINISTRIES

McKinney, Texas

Dedicated to the memory of

Tom Reich & Stancil Bynum

Two trustees of Lamb & Lion Ministries
who have been promoted to glory.

First edition, 2010

Copyright © 2010 by Lamb & Lion Ministries

ISBN: 978-0-945593-18-8

Library of Congress Control Number: 2010907479

Lamb & Lion Ministries
P.O. Box 919
McKinney, Texas 75070
lamblion@lamblion.com
www.lamblion.com

Cover design by Keith Fink of Master's Press in Dallas, Texas.
Heaven picture, "Welcome Home" © 2010 by Danny Hahlbohm.
Hell picture from Michelangelo's "Last Judgment."

All scripture quotations, unless otherwise noted,
are from the New American Standard Version,
© 1995 by the Lockman Foundation.

Printed in the United States of America.

Contents

Books by Dr. David R. Reagan

(Most of these have been published in foreign languages)

The Christ in Prophecy Study Guide (McKinney, TX: Lamb & Lion Ministries, 1987). Second edition in 2001.

Trusting God: Learning to Walk by Faith (Lafayette, LA: Huntington House, 1987). Second edition in 1994.

Jesus is Coming Again! (Eugene, OR: Harvest House, 1992).

The Master Plan: Making Sense of the Controversies Surrounding Bible Prophecy Today (Eugene, OR: Harvest House, 1993).

Living for Christ in the End Times (Green Forest, AR: New Leaf Press, 2000).

Wrath and Glory: Unveiling the Majestic Book of Revelation (Green Forest, AR: New Leaf Press, 2001).

America the Beautiful? The United States in Bible Prophecy (McKinney, TX: Lamb & Lion Ministries, 2003). Second edition in 2006. Third edition in 2009.

God's Plan for the Ages: The Blueprint of Bible Prophecy (McKinney, TX: Lamb & Lion Ministries, 2005).

Preface

What more important topic could there be than that of eternity? Every person who has ever lived or who is alive today has an eternal destiny of either Heaven or Hell.

Atheists deny this. Their greatest hope is that there is nothing after death. (What a hope!) But their denial of both Heaven and Hell is futile, and it violates our basic nature, for one of the instincts we are born with is the sense that there is something beyond this life.

The Bible says that God has "placed eternity in our hearts" (Ecclesiastes 3:11), just as He has given us an instinctive knowledge that He exists (Romans 1:19 and 2:14).

Accordingly, the Bible exhorts us to live with an eternal perspective (Psalm 139:24). We are to "set our minds on the things above, and not on the things that are on earth" (Colossians 3:2 and 1 John 2:15-16). We are warned not to fall in love with the world, nor the things of the world, because we are told that if we love the world, the love of God is not in us (1 John 2:15).

Yet the Church today is filled with professing Christians who are clinging to this world as if it were their only hope. Why is that?

I believe the bottom line cause is an ignorance of what God's Word has to say about the future. And that problem, in turn, is due to the fact that most pastors avoid teaching and preaching Bible prophecy.

Incredible Promises

Bible prophecy is full of glorious promises about the believer's future — so glorious, in fact, that the Apostle Paul was moved to write: "I consider that the sufferings of this present time are not worthy to be compared with the glory that is to be revealed to us" (Romans 8:18). That is a mouthful!

I know people who are suffering mightily in this life from emotional problems, physical handicaps, and diseases of various kinds. Yet Paul declares that no matter what we may suffer, it cannot be compared to the glorious blessings that await those who have put their trust in Jesus as their Lord and Savior.

Paul repeats this incredible thought in 1 Corinthians 2:9 where he states (NIV):

> No eye has seen,
> No ear has heard,
> No mind has conceived
> What God has prepared
> For those who love Him.

I can guarantee you one thing for sure: If you ever spend the time to search out the promises of God's Word for believers after they die, you will fall out of love with this wretched world and start yearning with all your heart for Heaven.

Instead of feeling comfortable with this world, you will sense that you are a pilgrim passing through an alien land en route to your true home, an eternal one in Heaven.

Why this book?

The purpose of this book is to challenge you to live with an eternal perspective. In the process, I hope you will become excited about God's promises for your future life after death.

And regarding death, I pray this book will liberate you from any fear of it.

Unless, of course, you are a person who has never received Jesus as your Lord and Savior. If that is your situation, then you should very much fear death and the consequences to follow.

All of us are destined one day to stand before our Creator and be judged of everything we have ever thought or said or done in this life (Ecclesiastes 12:14). If you have placed your faith in Jesus as your Lord and Savior, you will be viewed by God as innocent and worthy of Heaven, for your sins will have been forgiven and forgotten. But if you have put your trust in yourself and your good works, you will be found guilty and will be condemned to Hell.

Which will it be for you? Heaven or Hell?

Let's search God's Word for insights about eternity, and let's begin by examining your attitude about death.

Dr. David R. Reagan
Allen, Texas
Spring of 2010

ETERNITY

Heaven or Hell?

Leavin' On My Mind

A Song by Rusty Goodman

The old house I'm living in
Is needing repair.
The windows and the shutters
Are letting in the cold, cold air.
I say to myself "I'm gonna fix'em
When I can get the time."
But all I've been getting lately
Is leavin' on my mind.

So I guess I should be looking
For a better place to live,
But I can't seem to get excited
About the world and what it can give.
I couldn't care less if I could buy it all
With a solitary dime,
For what good would a world do me
With leavin' on my mind?

Chorus:
Lately all I've got is leavin' on my mind.
Seems that's all I'm thinkin' 'bout
Most of the time.
But soon and very soon
I'll leave my trouble far behind.
Lately I've got leavin,'
Leavin' on my mind.

Charles F. "Rusty" Goodman (1933 - 1990) was born in Alabama into a family of seven children. He learned to sing and play the guitar at a very young age and was an accomplished artist on the steel guitar at the age of 14. He began singing with his family, "The Happy Goodmans," at age 16.

Introduction

The Fear of Death

"[Jesus] became a human being, so that by going through death as a man He might destroy him who had the power of death, that is, the devil: and might also set free those who lived their whole lives a prey to the fear of death." — Hebrews 2:14-15 (*The New Testament in Modern English* by J.B. Phillips)

Most people do not like to think about death, much less discuss it. We dismiss it from our minds, assuring ourselves that it is in the far distant future.

I was reminded of this fact when I saw an interview on television of the founder of Microsoft, billionaire Bill Gates. He was asked why he had not made any major financial donations to charity up to that point in his life. He responded that he had lived only half his life and thus still had plenty of time to consider donations.

I immediately thought, "How does he know he has lived only half his life? He could be dead tomorrow." A few days later, during a trip to Europe, a person walked up to him and slammed him in the face with a pie! It occurred to me the person could just as easily have shot him.

In sharp contrast, I am reminded of a friend of mine, Ed Towne, who was the pastor of Pantano Christian Church in Tucson, Arizona during the 1980's. He was invited to come to the largest church in Washington State and preach on a

Sunday morning and evening. As he was driving to the church for the evening service, he was involved in a terrible auto crash that killed him instantly. The rescue squad found his Bible on the floor of his vehicle. In it was the sermon he was going to deliver that evening. The first sentence of the sermon read: "There is not one person here this evening who can say with certainty that he or she will be alive in the morning."

Facing the Reality of Death

The Bible says that life is like a vapor — here one moment and gone the next (James 4:14). In other places, it compares a lifetime to a mere breath (Job 7:7 and Psalm 39:5) or a passing shadow (Psalm 144:4).

But we do not like to face this reality. People nip and tuck their faces and cover them with cosmetics to camouflage their advancing age and its testimony to the inevitability of death. We refer to people "passing away," or "going home," or "kicking the bucket," or "cashing in the chips." The euphemisms go on and on. We find it almost impossible to simply say, "He died."

I had a terrible experience along this line many years ago when a friend of mine asked me to preside at her father's funeral. She was a professing Christian, so I was not at all prepared for the shock I was about to experience.

She asked me to accompany her to the funeral home to help her make all the plans for the memorial service. When we arrived, the funeral director told her that her father was ready for viewing and asked her if she would like to view his remains before sitting down to discuss the funeral service. She said she would.

He took us to the viewing room, and when she looked into the casket, she suddenly started screaming at the top of her voice, "He looks dead! He looks dead! He looks dead!"

I made the mistake of observing, "But he is dead!" That remark made her go ballistic. She began screaming, "I want him to look alive. Make him look alive!"

Very quickly several technicians showed up and started adjusting the lights and the cosmetics on the man's face. For the next few minutes they worked feverishly, trying their best to make a corpse look alive.

Experiencing the Fear of Death

The Bible says that most people live in life-long bondage to the fear of death (Hebrews 2:15). There is no doubt that statement is true.

Several years ago, a colleague of mine, Dennis Pollock, did some research about how people with a secular view of life have dealt with death. His findings were most revealing.[1]

Let me share two examples with you. The first is Raymond Burr, the actor who played the lawyer, Perry Mason, on television. Although he never lost a case in his TV dramas, he ended up losing his nerve on his deathbed. He was so frightened of death that he refused to sleep, for fear that he might not wake up. He sat up in his bed for more than 30 hours fighting sleep before exhaustion overcame him. He finally gave in, and he died within a few hours after he went to sleep.

The other example is that of Alfred Hitchcock, the great film director who played with death in his movies and television programs. But when it came his turn to meet the grim reaper, he fell apart emotionally and cried uncontrollably, telling Ingrid Bergman about his morbid fear of death.

Many other celebrity examples of the fear of death could be cited. Consider the great baseball player, Ted Williams. His wife had his body frozen so that it could be preserved in the hope that it might one day be brought back to life by some scientific development.[2] Woody Allen, the comedian and film director, summed it up best in his typically humorous way when he observed: "I'm not afraid of death. I just don't want to be there when it happens."[3]

In one of the oldest passages in the Bible, one of Job's friends characterized death as the "king of terrors" (Job 18:14). Even King David in one of his psalms referred to the "terrors of death" falling upon him (Psalm 55:4). He proceeded in the psalm to deal with the fear by placing his trust in God (Psalm 55:16), but in the process he expressed the kind of fear that grips most people when they are faced with death: "Fear and trembling come upon me, and horror has overwhelmed me" (Psalm 55:5).

Suppressing the Fear

Most of the time people are able to suppress their fear of death, but it is always there, just below the surface. It normally surfaces when a friend or family member dies, when a person experiences a near-death event like a serious auto accident, or when a person begins to reach middle age. And, of course, lying in a fox hole with bombs exploding all around always gives rise to thoughts of death!

I think one of the reasons the death of Princess Diana had such a great worldwide impact was because she was so young. When we are young we tend to think we are invincible and will live indefinitely. It is always sobering when we experience the death of a young person. It forces us to think about our own mortality, something that is most uncomfortable to do. But it never lasts long, because we are always anxious to put the whole topic in the back of our minds.

I saw this happen when I was a teenager. I was living in Waco, Texas in May of 1953 when the worst tornado in the history of the state hit the city. A total of 114 people were killed by the storm. The downtown area looked like it had been hit with an atomic bomb.

For weeks thereafter, the churches of Waco were filled to capacity as people tried to deal with the terror of the storm. But within about six months, attendance began to taper off, and before long, the churches were back to normal in their attendance.

Death is a fact that all people need to face and prepare for. The only people who are not going to experience death are those believers in Jesus Christ who are alive at the time He returns to take His Church out of this world in an event called the Rapture (1 Thessalonians 4:13-18). Those believers who die before that time will overcome death through the resurrection and glorification of their bodies.

Our Life Span

I have a very personal interest in the topic of death because, as I write this book, I am approaching the age of 72. That means I am living on borrowed time. I say that because the Bible says that "as for the days of our life, they contain 70 years, or if due to strength, 80 years" (Psalm 90:10).

We were originally intended to live forever in close communion with our Creator, sustaining our lives by feeding on the Tree of Life (Genesis 2:9 and 3:22). But when our first ancestors, Adam and Eve, sinned against the Lord, they were ejected from the Garden of Eden and denied access to the Tree of Life. Physical death became the penalty of sin, and the life span of Man was reduced to a thousand years.

As the decades and centuries passed, two things occurred that reduced this life span even further. One was the increasing corruption of the genetic code. The other was the great, worldwide flood of Noah's time which produced a relatively harsh post-flood ecosystem.

During the 400 years immediately following the flood, Mankind's life span fell drastically from an average of 912 years before the flood to 222 years.[4] Thereafter, life spans continued to gradually decline. Abraham, who was born 350 years after the flood, died at the age of 175 (Genesis 25:7). Moses was born 255 years after the death of Abraham and lived to be 120 (Deuteronomy 34:7). Joshua, Moses' successor lived 110 years (Judges 2:8). Ultimately Man's life span settled at 70 years. But the life *expectancy* of humans fell far more than that. It plunged to about 33 years.[5]

Yes, you read that correctly — 33 years. You see, throughout most of recorded history, life has been hard and short, characterized by a very high infant mortality rate, savage diseases, and brutal wars.

One result of this is that the population of the world remained relatively static for centuries. It is estimated by most demographers that the earth's population at the time of Jesus was 200 million at most. It took 1,400 years for that number to double. Humanity's population did not reach one billion until around 1850.[6]

The Medical Revolution

It was during the 20th Century that the population of the world took off like a rocket and started growing exponentially. At the beginning of the century, the world's population was 1.6 billion. By the end of the century, it was 6 billion. This explosive growth was due to the development of modern medicine. Most of the medical achievements that we take for granted today are relatively new:[7]

- 1862 — The germ theory of disease
- 1867 — Antiseptic surgical procedures
- 1895 — Discovery of X-Rays
- 1899 — Development of aspirin
- 1901 — Development of blood typing
- 1907 — First successful blood transfusion

- 1922 — First use of insulin to treat diabetes

- 1927 — First vaccine for tetanus

The most significant discovery is not included in the list above. It occurred in 1928 when penicillin was discovered.[8] That's right, the very first antibiotic was not discovered until 1928! The lack of such a medicine was one of the reasons that the flu pandemic of World War I resulted in over 40 million deaths worldwide. You see, the flu often produced pneumonia, and pneumonia led to death.

I was born in 1938, ten years after the discovery of penicillin. The timing of my birth was most propitious for me, because in 1950 I suffered a severe attack of appendicitis. If I had been born in the 19th Century, or even in the early 20th Century, I would have died at the age of 12.

This point was emphasized to me recently while I was reading a biographical sketch about the great Western artist, Frederick Remington.[9] He died in 1909 at the age of 48 from appendicitis. Similarly, I discovered in a biography of President Harry S Truman that his father died in 1914 from a simple hernia operation, which, of course, in those days was not simple.[10]

Today we rarely give any serious concern to maladies like appendicitis and pneumonia, but for most of the centuries of recorded history, these afflictions were major killers.

I could name several other times in my life when I would have died if I had been born a few years earlier. All of us living today are very fortunate to be able to look forward to life spans twice as long as our forefathers.

The Continuing Reality of Death

In 1900 the life expectancy of a man in the United States was 47 years. Today it is 75 years. For women, the life expectancy in 1900 was 51 years; today it is 80.[11] Because we have experienced such a radical increase in longevity during the past 100 years, most of us today tend to take the reality of death much less seriously than people in previous centuries.

But death is still a reality that we all must face.

Today, 146,357 people die worldwide every day. That translates into 102 per minute, 6,120 per hour, and 53.4 million per year.[12]

At age 71 I am rapidly approaching my appointment with death, assuming I achieve the current American life expectancy of 75 years for a man. But then, of course, I could die today or tomorrow, and so could you. Life is transitory. It is here one moment and gone the next. Again, it is like a vapor (James 4:13-15):

> Come, now, you who say," Today or tomorrow, we shall go to such a city, and spend a year there and engage in business and make a profit."

> Yet you do not know what your life will be like tomorrow. You are just a vapor that appears for a little while and then wanders away.

> Instead, you ought to say, "If the Lord wills, we shall live and also do this or that."

Attitudes Toward Death

As I near the end of my life, I do so without any fear because I am absolutely confident of my eternal destiny. That's because I accepted Jesus Christ as my Lord and Savior when I was 11 years old.

What about you? Do you fear death? Do you feel uncomfortable even thinking about it? Perhaps you believe this life is all there is and that death means annihilation. Or, do you suspect it could be the door to a very uncertain eternity?

One thing is for certain: If you have never received Jesus as your Lord and Savior, you should greatly fear death. This book will make that fact abundantly clear. You are going to discover that each of us has an eternal destiny and that it will be either Heaven or Hell. What eternal fate do you face?

Let's take a look at the only authoritative source on the subject — namely, the Word of God.

The Open Door

A Poem by Grace Coolidge

You, my son.
Have shown me God.
Your kiss upon my cheek
Has made me feel the gentle touch
Of Him who leads us on.

The memory of your smile, when young,
Reveals His face,
As mellowing years come on apace.
And when you went before,
You left the gates of Heaven ajar
That I might glimpse,
Approaching from afar,
The glories of His grace.

Hold, son, my hand,
Guide me along the path,
That, coming
I may stumble not
Nor roam,
Nor fail to show the way
Which leads us — home.

This poem, by President Calvin Coolidge's wife, was written on the fifth anniversary of the death of their son, Calvin Coolidge, Jr. He died at the age of 16 in July of 1924 of blood poisoning, just 11 months after his father had become President of the United States.

Chapter 1

What Happens When You Die?

"If a man dies, will he live again?"
— Job 14: 14 (NASV)

If several years ago you had asked me what happens when you die, I would have given you a pathetic answer.

I would have told you that when you die your soul goes to sleep until the Lord returns. At the return of the Lord, your soul is resurrected and judged, and you are either consigned to Hell or allowed to enter Heaven.

My conception of Heaven was that of a spirit world where the saved spend eternity as disembodied spirits, floating around on clouds, playing harps.

A Mistaken View

Needless to say, I couldn't get very excited about all that. I sure didn't like the idea of being unconscious in the grave for eons of time. Nor could I develop any enthusiasm for the prospect of being a disembodied spirit with no particular identity or personality. And the idea of playing a harp for all eternity was downright scandalous, for I had been taught that instrumental music in worship was an abomination!

You can imagine, therefore, the sense of shock I felt when I started studying Bible prophecy and discovered that all these ideas of mine about life after death were foreign to God's Word. But my shock quickly gave way to exhilaration when I discovered what the Lord really has in store for me.

The Biblical View

I learned from God's Word that when those of us who are Christians die, our spirits never lose their consciousness (Philippians 1:21-23 and 2 Corinthians 5:8). Instead, our fully conscious spirits are immediately ushered into the presence of Jesus by His holy angels (Luke 16:22).

Our spirits remain in the Lord's presence until He appears for His Church. At that time, He brings our spirits with Him, resurrects our bodies, reunites our spirits with our bodies, and then glorifies our bodies, perfecting them and rendering them eternal (1 Thessalonians 4:13-18).

We return with Him to Heaven in our glorified bodies where we are judged for our works to determine our degrees of rewards (2 Corinthians 5:10). When this judgment is completed, we participate in a glorious wedding feast to celebrate the union of Jesus and His Bride, the Church (Revelation 19:7-9).

Witnesses of Glory

At the conclusion of the feast, we burst from the heavens with Jesus, returning with Him to the earth in glory (Revelation 19:14). We witness His victory at Armageddon, we shout "Hallelujah!" as He is crowned King of kings and Lord of lords, and we revel in His glory as He begins to reign over all the earth from Mt. Zion in Jerusalem (Zechariah 14:1-9 and Revelation 19: 17-21).

For a thousand years we participate in that reign, assisting Him with the instruction, administration, and enforcement of His perfect laws (Daniel 7:13-14, 18, 27 and Revelation 20:1-6). We see the earth regenerated and nature reconciled (Isaiah 11:6-9). We see holiness abound and the earth flooded with peace, righteousness and justice (Micah 4:1-7).

At the end of the Lord's millennial reign, we witness the release of Satan to deceive the nations. We see the truly despicable nature of the heart of Man as millions rally to Satan in his attempt to overthrow the throne of Jesus. But we will shout "Hallelujah!" again when we witness God's supernatural destruction of Satan's armies and see Satan himself cast into Hell where he will be tormented forever (Revelation 20:7-10).

We will next witness the Great White Throne Judgment when the unrighteous are resurrected to stand before God. We will see perfect holiness and justice in action as God pronounces His terrible judgment upon this congregation of the damned who have rejected His gift of love and mercy in Jesus Christ (Revelation 20:11-13).

Jesus will be fully vindicated as every knee shall bow and every tongue confess that He is Lord. Then the unrighteous will receive their just reward as they are cast into Hell (Revelation 20:14-15).

Witnesses of a New Creation

We will then witness the most spectacular fireworks display in all of history.

We will be taken to the New Jerusalem, the eternal mansion prepared by Jesus for His Bride, and from there we will watch as God renovates this earth with fire, burning away all the filth and pollution left by Satan's last battle (2 Peter 3:12-13).

Just as the angels rejoiced when God created the universe, we will rejoice as we watch God superheat this earth and reshape it like a hot ball of wax into the New Earth, the eternal earth, the paradise where we will live forever in the presence of God (Revelation 21:1-7).

What a glorious moment it will be when we are lowered to the New Earth inside the fabulous New Jerusalem (Revelation 21:2). God will come down from Heaven to dwell with us (Revelation 21:3). He will proclaim: "Behold,

I make all things new" (Revelation 21:5). We will see God face to face (Revelation 22:4). He will wipe away all our tears (Revelation 21:4). Death will be no more (Revelation 21:4). We will be given new names (Revelation 2:17), and we will exist as individual personalities encased in perfect bodies (Philippians 3:21). And we will grow eternally in knowledge and love of our infinite Creator, honoring Him with our talents and gifts.

Now, I can get excited about that!

The Word vs. Tradition

Isn't it amazing how far we can drift away from the Word of God when we stop reading His Word and start mouthing the traditions of Men?

As I kept making one discovery after another in God's Prophetic Word that ran contrary to what I had been taught, I began to wonder about the origin of the doctrines I had learned. It didn't take me long to discover that the source was Greek philosophy.

The first attempt to mix the concepts of Greek philosophy with the teachings of God's Word came very early in the history of the Church. The attempt was called Gnosticism. The Gnostic heresy arose among the first Gentile converts because they tried to Hellenize the Scriptures; that is, they tried to make the Scriptures conform to the basic tenets of Greek philosophy.

The Greeks believed that the material universe, including the human body, was evil. This negative view of the creation was diametrically opposed to Hebrew thought, as revealed in the Bible. To the Hebrew mind, the world was created good (Genesis 1:31). And even though the goodness of the creation was corrupted by the sin of Man (Isaiah 24:5-6), the creation still reflects to some degree the glory of God (Psalm 19:1). Most important, the creation will someday be redeemed by

God (Romans 8:18-23).

The Gnostic Heresy

When the first Gentiles were converted to the Gospel, their Greek mind-set immediately collided with some of the fundamental teachings of Christianity. For example, they wondered, "How could Jesus have come in the flesh if He was God? God is holy. How can He who is holy be encased in a body which is evil?"

In short, because they viewed the material universe as evil, they could not accept the Bible's teaching that God became incarnate in the flesh. Their response was to develop the Gnostic heresy that Jesus was a spirit being or phantom who never took on the flesh and therefore never experienced physical death.

This heresy is denounced strongly in Scripture. In 1 John 4:1-2 we are told to test those who seek our spiritual fellowship by asking them to confess "that Jesus Christ has come in the flesh."

The Augustinian Corruption

About 400 A.D. a remarkable theologian by the name of Saint Augustine attempted to Hellenize what the Scriptures taught about end time events and life after death. Augustine was very successful in his attempt. His views were adopted by the Council of Ephesus in 431 A.D. and have remained Catholic dogma to this day.

The influence of Greek philosophy would not allow Augustine to accept what the Bible taught about life after death. For example, the Bible says the saints will spend eternity in glorified bodies on a New Earth (Revelation 21:1-7). Such a concept was anathema to the Greek mind of Augustine. If the material world is evil, then he reasoned that the material world must cease to exist when the Lord returns. Augustine solved the problem by spiritualizing what the Bible said. He did this by arguing that the "new earth" of Revelation 21 is just symbolic language for Heaven.

Augustine's views are held by most professing Christians today, both Catholic and Protestant. That means that most of Christianity today teaches Greek philosophy rather than the Word of God when it comes to the realm of end time prophecy and life after death.

The Intermediate State

Some of the greatest confusion about life after death relates to the intermediate state between death and eternity. Some people advocate a concept called "soul sleep." They argue that both the saved and unsaved are unconscious after death until the return of Jesus.

But the Bible makes it crystal clear that our spirit does not lose its consciousness at death. The only thing that "falls asleep" is our body — in a symbolic sense. Paul says in 2 Corinthians 5:8 that he would prefer to be "absent from the body and at home with the Lord." In Philippians 1:21 he observes, "For me to live is Christ and to die is gain." He then adds in verse 23 that his desire is "to depart and be with Christ." Paul certainly did not expect to be in a coma after he died!

If then our spirits retain their consciousness after death, where do they go? The Bible teaches that prior to the resurrection of Jesus, the spirits of the dead went to a place called Hades ("Sheol" in the Old Testament). The spirits existed there consciously in one of two compartments, either Paradise or Torments. This concept is pictured graphically in Jesus' story of the rich man and Lazarus (Luke 16:19-31).

The Bible indicates that after the death of Jesus on the Cross, He descended into Hades to declare the good news that He had shed His blood for the sins of Mankind (1 Peter 3:18-19 and 4:6). The Bible also indicates that after His resurrection, when He ascended into Heaven, Jesus took Paradise with Him, transferring the spirits of dead saints from Hades to Heaven (Ephesians 4:8-9 and 2 Corinthians 12:1-4). The spirits of dead saints are thereafter pictured as being in Heaven before the throne of God (See Revelation 6:9 and 7:9).

Paul confirms that Paradise was moved to Heaven in 2 Corinthians 12:1-4 where he says he was "caught up to the third heaven" where God resides. He then refers to this place as Paradise.

The spirits of the righteous dead could not go directly to Heaven before the Cross because their sins were not forgiven. Instead, their sins were merely covered by their faith. The forgiveness of their sins had to await the shedding of the blood of the Messiah (Leviticus 17:11; Romans 5:8-9, and Hebrews 9:22).

But since the time of the Cross, those who die in the Lord are taken directly to Heaven because today, when a person receives Jesus as Lord and Savior, that person's sins are forgiven and forgotten. The state of the lost, however, is still the same as it has always been. Their spirits go to Hades, to the compartment called Torments, where they await their ultimate judgment and confinement to Hell.

The Intermediate Body

During the intermediate state, between death and resurrection, what is the nature of the existence of the saved and lost? Do they become pure spirit in nature? The answer is no, not at all.

God alone is spirit (John 4:24). Man, like the angels, was created to have a body. As Paul puts it in 2 Corinthians 5:3, we "shall not be found naked."

When we shed our mortal bodies in death, with the separation of the spirit from the body, the Bible clearly teaches that we receive an intermediate spirit body — intermediate between our current mortal body and the immortal body we will receive at the time we are resurrected. Evidence of this fact can be found in several places in the Bible.

- When King Saul wanted to know how he would fare in an upcoming battle, he went to a witch at Endor and asked her to call up Samuel from the dead so that he could consult with him. Evidently thinking that her familiar demon spirit would appear, the witch was astonished when Samuel appeared instead and proceeded to condemn Saul for trafficking in the occult (1 Samuel 28:7-19). Both she and Saul immediately recognized Samuel when he appeared.

- When Jesus told the story of Lazarus and the Rich man, he made it clear that they fully recognized each other after they died and their spirits went to Hades, Lazarus to the compartment called Paradise, and the Rich man to the compartment called Torments. Their spirits were incorporated into identifiable bodies (Luke 16:19-31).

- At His transfiguration, Jesus was joined by Moses and Elijah, and the apostles who were present were able to recognize both men as they talked with Jesus (Matthew 17:1-7).

- When the Apostle John was taken up to Heaven, he saw an immense multitude of people in white robes standing before the throne of God with palm branches in their hands. When he asked who they were, he was told that they were martyrs coming out of the Great Tribulation (Revelation 7:9-15).

In each of these cases, we see dead people whose spirits have been incorporated into recognizable bodies that are clothed.

A Summary

So, what happens when you die? If you are a child of God, your spirit is immediately ushered into the bosom of Jesus by His holy angels. You are given an intermediate spirit body, and you remain in Heaven, in the presence of God, until the time of the Rapture. When Jesus comes for His Church, He brings your spirit with Him, resurrects your body and puts your spirit back into that body. He then glorifies your body, making it eternal in nature (1 Corinthians 15 and 1 Thessalonians 4). You reign with Jesus for a thousand years and then live eternally with Him on the new earth (Revelation 20-22).

If you are not a child of God, then your spirit goes to Hades at your death where you exist in an intermediate spirit body. This is a place of torments where you are held captive until the resurrection of the unrighteous which takes place at the end of the millennial reign of Jesus. At that resurrection you are taken before the Great White Throne of God where you are judged by your works and then condemned to the "second death," which is the "lake of fire" or Hell (Revelation 20:11-15).

Preparing for Eternity

One thing is certain: "Every knee shall bow and every tongue confess that 'Jesus is Lord!'" (Isaiah 45:23 and Romans 14:11). Your eternal destiny will be determined by when you make this confession.

If it is made before you die, then you will spend eternity with God. If not, then you will make the confession at the Great White Throne judgment before you are cast into Hell. To spend eternity with God, your confession of Jesus as Lord must be made *now*.

> "If you confess with your mouth Jesus as Lord, and believe in your heart that God raised Him from the dead, you shall be saved." — Romans 10:9

Questions about Death

1) What about reincarnation? Didn't Jesus teach reincarnation when He said a person cannot enter Heaven unless he is "born again"? (John 3:3)

This is an important question since surveys have shown that 25% of professing Christians and 50% of all people worldwide believe in reincarnation.

Let's begin with a definition of reincarnation. It is the belief that a person's soul must live a succession of lives over a long period of time. The purpose of each reincarnation is to further purify the soul until it reaches perfection, at which point the soul is absorbed into the Divine Spirit from which it has been alienated.

Dr. Ray Pritchard, pastor of Calvary Memorial Church in Oak Park, Illinois, has described reincarnation as "a kind of self-salvation worked out over the eons of time."[1]

A second element to this doctrine is a belief in the essential divinity of the individual. It is, therefore, an expression of the pantheistic concept that everyone and everything is God.

Reincarnation is a characteristic belief of most Eastern religions like Hinduism and Buddhism. It is also characteristic of primitive, animistic religions that worship nature.

The concept began to gain acceptance in the Western world in the mid-20th Century with the rise of the New Age Movement. It was popularized in the United States in the writings of the movie actress, Shirley MacLaine. In her book, *Dancing in the Light*, she wrote: "I know that I exist, therefore, I AM. I know that the God source exists, therefore IT IS. Since I am part of the force, then I AM that I AM."[2]

The concept of reincarnation is totally unbiblical. The Bible declares that "it is appointed for men to die once, and after this comes judgment" (Hebrews 9:27). Jesus taught the same thing when He said: "An hour is coming, in which all who are in the tombs shall hear His voice, and shall come forth; those who did the good deeds to a resurrection of life, those who committed the evil deeds to a resurrection of judgment" (John 5:28-29). We live, we die, and we face judgment. There is no mention of reincarnation because it is a myth.

The whole concept of reincarnation also violates the fundamental biblical principle that we are saved by grace through faith and not by works (Ephesians 2:8-10). No person can save himself by being good. We are to look to the incarnation of Jesus for our hope, not our reincarnation.

Finally, as to Jesus' statement that we must be "born again," He was speaking of spiritual rebirth, not physical. Jesus makes this crystal clear in the verses that follow this statement (John 3:4-7).

2) Where does Purgatory fit into the sequence of events following death?

Purgatory is another mythical concept that is foreign to the Bible. Even those who believe in the concept admit that there is no biblical basis for it,[3] but they argue that it makes common sense that sinful men must be purged of their sins before they can have eternal fellowship with the Holy God who created them.

Accordingly, Catholic doctrine teaches that the souls of the saved must experience Purgatory when they die in order to be purged of their sins through a process of pain and suffering. It is also taught that the duration of those in Purgatory can be shortened by actions of the living in the form of prayers, masses, the lighting of candles, and the saying of the Rosary.

There is no doubt that we need to be purged of our sins, but the Bible teaches that the blood of Christ is sufficient to cleanse us from all sin (1 John 1:7). No other purging is necessary. To argue otherwise is to blaspheme the blood of Jesus.

The whole argument about Purgatory boils down to whether or not your faith is in the grace of God through the atonement work of Jesus, or whether your faith has been placed in your own works. If you are trusting in your works, then you need Purgatory, but it occurred at the Cross two thousand years ago. It is not a future event that occurs after death.

3) Is it wrong to have your body cremated after death?

This is an area of heated opinions among Bible believing Christians.

Those opposed to cremation argue that historically it has been a pagan practice which shows no respect for the body or for the biblical promise that one day it will be resurrected.

Those who support cremation point out that the Bible is silent about the issue and therefore Christians should have the freedom to decide the matter according to the dictates of their consciences (Romans 14:1-12), without condemning each other.

There is no doubt that the weight of Christian tradition favors burial, but the Bible nowhere explicitly condemns cremation. And, of course, there are those who have been unintentionally cremated as they died in fires, just as there are those whose bodies have been subjected to destruction through drowning in the ocean.

All bodies will be miraculously reconstructed at their time of resurrection. Keep in mind that the One who will call the bodies of the dead to come forth from tombs, ashes, dust, and oceans is the same One who spoke the whole universe into existence.

In an excellent article on the subject that appeared in *Christianity Today* magazine, the author, Timothy George (Dean of the Beeson Divinity School at Samford University) made the following insightful observation: "The real question for Christians is not whether one is buried or cremated, but the meaning given to these acts."[4]

His point is a good one. Burial practices can be bizarre, as with mummification or the dressing up of a corpse in a fancy tuxedo to be placed in an air-tight expensive coffin. Likewise, cremation can be treated as if one were burning trash, with no respect being given to the ashes.

I personally have requested that if I die before the Rapture occurs, I would like to be cremated and have my ashes scattered on the Mount of Olives in Jerusalem. The reason is that Zechariah 14 teaches that when the Messiah returns, He will come to the pinnacle of that mount.

This is the reason that the Mount of Olives is covered with tens of thousands of graves. Orthodox Jews believe the prophecy of Zechariah 14, and they desire to be buried on the mount so that they will be among the first to be resurrected. Gentiles cannot be buried there. But I know of at least one who is.

Back in 1999 a dear friend of mine, Clem Stewart, decided that he wanted to go with me on a pilgrimage I was leading to the Holy Land. Three months before we were scheduled to leave, Clem drowned while on a fishing trip. His wife and daughter made the trip with me and brought along his ashes. We conducted a memorial service on the slope of the Mount of Olives and scattered his ashes there under a fig tree. It was a beautiful service that affirmed Clem's faith in his resurrection, and I believe it brought honor and glory to the Lord.

4) What do you think of "near-death" experiences?

I do not give them much credence.

For one thing, nearly all of them report pleasant experiences of serenity in the midst of a bright angelic being — regardless of their spiritual condition when they supposedly died.

Since the Bible clearly teaches that our eternal destiny is either Heaven or Hell, it makes no sense that those who are spiritually lost would have beautiful experiences of contentment after death. Furthermore, it should be kept in mind that the Scriptures say that Satan can disguise himself as "an angel of light" (2 Corinthians 11:14).

I am even more skeptical of those who claim that they visited Heaven or Hell and were sent back to tell us about these places. I believe the Bible contains all the information we need about both of these places.

I am reminded of Jesus's story about the rich man and Lazarus (Luke 16:19-31). Both died and went to Hades, the rich man to a compartment called Torments and Lazarus to one called Paradise. As the rich man suffered torment, he saw Abraham far away and cried out to him, asking him to send Lazarus back to warn his relatives, lest they also end up in torment. Abraham answered: "They have Moses and the Prophets [the Word of God]; let them hear them."

The rich man persisted: "No, father Abraham, but if someone goes to them from the dead, they will repent."

Abraham's chilling response was: "If they do not listen to Moses and the Prophets, they will not be persuaded even if someone rises from the dead."

Later, this statement by Abraham was proved — first with the resuscitation of Jesus' friend, Lazarus, and second with the resurrection of Jesus Himself.

The resuscitation of Lazarus was spectacular (John 11:1-47). Lazarus had been dead for four days when Jesus called him to come forth from his tomb. The miracle could not be refuted. Yet the spiritual leaders of Israel reacted by conspiring to put Jesus to death (John 11:47-53).

The evidence of the resurrection of Jesus was even more overwhelming. His body disappeared from His tomb despite the fact that the tomb was sealed with a large stone and was put under the guard of Roman soldiers (Matthew 27:65-66). Further, Jesus made post-resurrection appearances to many people in many different places (1 Corinthians 15:5-8). Yet the spiritual leaders of the Jews still refused to believe.

5) Could it be possible that the souls of the lost are simply annihilated at death?

This is the teaching of the Jehovah's Witnesses and other cultic groups. Those who hold this view usually try to substantiate it with Ecclesiastes 9:5 which says, "For the living know they will die; but the dead do not know anything, nor have they any longer a reward, for their memory is forgotten."

To base any doctrine on a verse in Ecclesiastes is dangerous because most of the book is about the vanity of Man and is written from Man's perspective. Thus, this verse appears to be stating that from a fatalistic human perspective, the dead have ceased to exist and are conscious of nothing.

It is also dangerous to base any doctrine on just one verse without taking into consideration what the rest of the Bible says. Again, in His story about Lazarus and the rich man (Luke 16:19-31), Jesus clearly teaches the continuing existence of both the saved and lost and the consciousness of both. And in Revelation 20, we are taught that at the end of the Lord's millennial reign, all those who died in a lost condition will be resurrected, judged, and consigned to Hell (Revelation 20:1-15).

6) How can you say there is no soul sleep after death when the Bible often refers to death as "sleep"? See: Job 14:12, Daniel 12:2, John 11:11-13, 1 Corinthians 11:30, and 1 Corinthians 15:51.

Sleep is used as a metaphor for death because the dead body does "sleep" in the sense that it will one day be "awakened" when it is resurrected.

But the spirit never loses its consciousness. Again, this is illustrated in Jesus's story about the rich man and Lazarus (Luke 16:19-31). Also, in Revelation 7:9-15 the martyrs of the Great Tribulation are pictured in Heaven in spirit bodies wearing white robes, worshiping the Lord, and serving Him day and night.

7) When will death cease? And will its cessation apply only to Man or to all the creation?

Death came into the world shortly after the creation week when Adam and Eve sinned against God, and it affected all of creation — including plants and animals (Genesis 3:14-24). Also, as part of God's punishment for sin, a curse was placed upon all the creation.

Before the curse, Man lived in perfect harmony with the creation. He was master of all (Genesis 1:28). There were no poisonous plants or carnivorous animals. Nor were there any natural disasters. All was perfect (Genesis 1:31).

But with Man's sin came death and the curse. All the creation was thrown askew. Man had to strive against nature to make his living. Poisonous plants and weeds appeared. Some of the animals became meat-eaters and thus presented a threat to Mankind. Natural disasters began. Ever since that time, the creation has been in bondage to decay (Romans 8:20).

The good news is that the moment God placed the curse upon His creation, He promised that one day it would be lifted and all the creation would be redeemed through "the seed of woman" (Genesis 3:15). Jesus, who was born of a virgin, became that seed of woman.

The promised redemption occurred at the Cross, but its application to death and the creation has been delayed until the Lord's return (Hebrews 2:8). The Bible teaches that the restoration will begin with the return of Jesus. That's the reason Paul pictures all the creation yearning for the return of the Messiah (Romans 8:19-22), and it's the reason that Peter, in his second sermon, proclaimed that the return of Jesus would herald the "restoration of all things" (Acts 3:21).

When Jesus returns, and His millennial reign begins, the curse will be lifted. The animal kingdom will be restored to peace as the wolf will dwell with the lamb and the lion will eat straw with the ox (Isaiah 11:6-7). Peace will also be restored between Man and the animal kingdom, and thus children will play with lions and snakes (Isaiah 11:6-9). And Man will no longer have to strive against nature. "Waters will break forth in the wilderness" (Isaiah 35:6), and the agricultural production of the earth will be greatly multiplied (Joel 2:24-25 and Amos 9:13).

Death will be continued during the Millennium, but it will be curtailed. The saved who go into the Millennium in the flesh, will have their lives extended for the duration: "For as the lifetime of a tree, so shall be the days of My people" (Isaiah 65:22). Those born during the Millennium and who accept Jesus as their Lord and Savior, will also have their lives extended, but those who do not will be subject to death (Isaiah 65:20).

The restoration of God's creation will be culminated at the conclusion of the millennial reign, when this earth is renovated with fire, producing a perfected New Earth where the saved will live eternally in the presence of God. Death will be abolished (Revelation 21:4), and the curse will no longer exist (Revelation 22:3).

8) Will people be given a second chance after death to accept Jesus as their Lord and Savior?

The answer is a firm no! Where you spend eternity is a choice you must make in this life. The Bible says that "it is appointed for men to die once and after this comes judgment" (Hebrews 9:27).

The Bible does teach that when the lost are judged that every one of them will bow their knee and confess that Jesus is Lord (Isaiah 45:23, Romans 14:10-12 and Philippians 2:9-11). That will be some scene to witness! Think of it, every vile atheist who has ever lived will acknowledge Jesus as God in the flesh, as will every nefarious person like Stalin and Hitler. But it will be too late. Their eternal fate will already be sealed.

If you want to live eternally with your Creator, you must accept His Son as your Lord and Savior in this life. Jesus paid the price for your reconciliation with God at the Cross when He died for your sins (Romans 5:8-11). You must reach out in faith and receive that gift by accepting Jesus as your Lord and Savior (John 3:16 and Romans 10:9).

9) How should a Christian face death?

With confidence, viewing it as a door to eternal life with God the Father.

In this regard, two great preachers come to mind: Dwight L. Moody and Martyn Lloyd-Jones. Dwight Moody (1837-1899) was the best known American evangelist of the 19th Century. Speaking of his death, he said, "Folks, someday you will hear the news that Dwight L. Moody is dead. Don't you believe it. I shall be more alive than I ever was!"

Martyn Lloyd-Jones (1899-1981) was one of the most respected preachers of Britain during the 20th Century. As he lay dying, he lapsed into a coma. In the days following, his relatives gathered from all over Europe to be with him when he died. He suddenly awoke from the coma, looked around the room at all the people gathered around his bed, and said, "I don't want anyone praying for my recovery. I am ready to meet my Lord."

The difference in the hope between a believer and an unbeliever is summed up well in two famous epitaphs. One is found on a tombstone in a cemetery in Thurmont, Maryland: "Here lies an atheist, all dressed up and no place to go!" The other is the one that Benjamin Franklin wrote for himself:

> The body of B. Franklin, printer (like the cover of an old book, its contents torn out and stript of its lettering and gilding) lies here, food for worms. But the work shall not be lost; for it will (as he believed) appear once more in a new and more elegant edition, revised and corrected by the Author.

After the Shadows

A Hymn by James Rowe

After the midnight, morning will greet us;
After the sadness, joy will appear;
After the tempest, sunlight will meet us;
After the jeering, praise we shall hear.

After the battle, peace will be given;
After the weeping, song there will be;
After the journey there will be Heaven,
Burdens will fall and we shall be free.

Refrain:

After the shadows, there will be sunshine;
After the frown, the soul-cheering smile;
Cling to the Savior, love Him forever;
All will be well in a little while.

James Rowe (1865-1933) was born in Devonshire, England, the son of a copper miner. After working for the Irish government for four years, James emigrated to the United States in 1889 at the age of 24. He settled in Albany, New York, where he worked for railroad companies for ten years, before becoming an inspector for the Hudson River Humane Society. He then worked for music publishers in Texas and Tennessee. He spent his final years in Vermont working with his daughter, an artist, writing verses for greeting cards. James wrote the words to many hymns during his lifetime. Perhaps his best known hymn is "Love Lifted Me."

Chapter 2

What About Resurrection and Judgment?

"Fear God and keep His commandments . . .
For God will bring every act to judgment,
everything which is hidden, whether it is good
or evil." — Ecclesiastes 12:13-14 (NASV)

My boyhood church always taught that there would be one resurrection and one judgment. Everyone who had ever lived would be resurrected at one time, and all of us — the just and the unjust — would be judged at the same time. The sheep would be separated from the goats at the Great White Throne Judgment pictured in Revelation 20:11-15.

Another thing we were taught about this judgment was something very frightening. We were told that none of us would have any idea whether we would be saved or lost until this judgment took place. Preachers would paint vivid word pictures of how nervous each of us would be as we awaited our turn for judgment. Our hearts would be pounding in anticipation as we waited for the final pronouncement of "Saved!" or "Lost!"

But these concepts are all wrong. The Bible reveals that there will be more than one resurrection and more than one judgment. The Bible also makes it clear that you can know in this life whether or not you are saved. You will not have to wait for your judgment before God to learn your eternal destiny.

Multiple Resurrections

Concerning resurrection, Jesus clearly taught that there would be more than one resurrection. In John 5:29 He refers to a "resurrection of life" and a "resurrection of judgment." The apostle Paul confirmed this concept in his defense before Felix when he stated that he believed the teaching of the prophets "that there shall certainly be a resurrection of both the righteous and the wicked" (Acts 24:15).

Of course, it could be argued that the two resurrections referred to in these scriptures will occur at the same time. Thus, if they were to happen simultaneously, there would, in effect, be only one resurrection. However, the Scriptures establish the fact that the resurrections will be separate and that the resurrection of the righteous will occur in stages.

In other words, the Bible does not teach one resurrection or even two resurrections in *number*. Rather, it teaches that there will be two resurrections in *type* which will be conducted in stages, resulting in several resurrections — at least four, to be specific.

The Resurrection of the Just

That the resurrection of the righteous will occur in stages is clearly taught in 1 Corinthians 15:20-23:

> 20) But now Christ has been raised from the dead, the first fruits of those who are asleep.

> 21) For since by a man came death, by a man also came the resurrection of the dead.

> 22) For as in Adam all die, so also in Christ all will be made alive.

> 23) But each in his own order: Christ the first fruits, after that those who are Christ's at His coming . . .

As you can see from this passage, the first stage of the resurrection of the righteous has already happened, for verse 20 says that "Christ has been raised from the dead, the first fruits of those who are asleep."

Verses 22 and 23 go on to explain that all who have died in Christ shall be made alive, "but each in his own order: Christ, the first fruits, after that those who are Christ's at His coming."

The imagery of the harvest that is used in these verses is a key to understanding the first resurrection — the resurrection of the righteous.

The Harvest Imagery

In Bible times the harvest was conducted in three stages. It began with the gathering of the first fruits which were offered as a sacrifice of thanksgiving to God (Exodus 34:26).

It proceeded with the general harvest. But not all was taken in this harvest. Some of the crop was left in the field to be gathered by the poor and the needy. This was called the gleanings (Leviticus 19:9-10).

Using this imagery, the Bible presents the resurrection of Jesus as the "first fruits" of the resurrection of the righteous. The gathering of the Church Age saints, living and dead, which will occur before the Tribulation at the time of the Rapture, is thus the general harvest stage of the resurrection of the righteous (John 14:1-3 and 1 Thessalonians 4:13-18).

But there is a third and final stage to this resurrection of the righteous. It is the gleanings, and it occurs at the end of the Tribulation when the Lord's Second Coming takes place. At that time two final groups of the righteous will be resurrected: the Tribulation martyrs (Revelation 20:4), and the Old Testament saints (Daniel 12:2).

The Resurrection of Old Testament Saints

Some people are startled by the thought that the Old Testament saints will not be resurrected until the end of the Tribulation. Many assume they will be included in the Rapture.

But keep in mind that the Rapture is a promise to the Church, and the Church only. It is pictured in the Scriptures as the Bridegroom coming for His Bride, the Church (Matthew 25:1-13).

Also, the book of Daniel makes it clear that the Old Testament saints will be resurrected at the end of the "time of distress" (Daniel 12:1-2).

A Summary of the Resurrection of the Just

The first resurrection, the resurrection of the righteous, occurs in three stages. It began with the resurrection of Jesus. It will continue at the Rapture with the resurrection of the Church Age saints. It will culminate at the Second Coming of Jesus with the resurrection of the Tribulation martyrs and the Old Testament saints.

See the chart on the next page for an illustration of the timing of these resurrections.

The Resurrection of the Unjust

The second type of resurrection, "the resurrection of the wicked" (Acts 24:15), will take place all at one time at the end of the millennial reign of Jesus. This is at the time of the Great White Throne Judgment, the judgment of the damned (Revelation 20:11-15).

Every person who ever failed to relate to God in faith will be resurrected at this time, regardless of when he or she may have lived and died — whether before or after the Cross. This resurrection will also include the unjust who died during the Tribulation and the Millennium.

The Sequence of Resurrections in the End Times

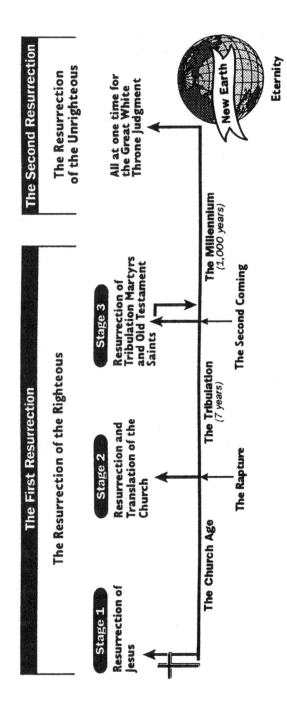

There will be no need for an additional resurrection of the righteous at the end of the Millennium, because all those born during that time who accept Jesus as their Savior will live to the end of the Lord's reign (Isaiah 65:19-20). "'As the lifetime of a tree, so shall be the days of My people,'. . . says the Lord" (Isaiah 65:22). In other words, life spans during the Millennium will be returned to what they were at the beginning of time, before the flood.

The Certainty of Judgment

Resurrection will be followed by judgment. Solomon wrote, "Fear God and keep His commandments . . . For God will bring every act to judgment, everything which is hidden, whether it is good or evil" (Ecclesiastes 12:13-14).

The apostle Paul emphasized the certainty of judgment. In Romans 2:16 he wrote, "God will judge the secrets of men through Christ Jesus." And in Romans 14:10, 12 he stated, "We shall all stand before the judgment seat of God . . . So then each one of us shall give account of himself to God." The writer to the Hebrews summed it up succinctly: "It is appointed for men to die once and after this comes judgment" (Hebrews 9:27).

The Completed Judgment

But not all people are going to be judged at the same time. Just as there are going to be several resurrections, there are also going to be several judgments.

One judgment has already taken place. It is the judgment of believers for their sins.

This comes as a surprise to most Christians. Some find it hard to believe. I'll never forget when I realized it from my study of Scripture. I became filled with so much joy that I felt like jumping pews all day!

Let me put it to you in another way. If you are truly born again, then you will never stand before the Lord and be judged of your sins. That's because the judgment for your sins took place at the Cross.

You see, all your sins, and mine, were placed upon Jesus as He hung upon the Cross, and the wrath we deserve was poured out upon Him (2 Corinthians 5:21). He became our substitute. He took our judgment for sin (Romans 8:3 and Galatians 3:13).

If you have appropriated the blood of Jesus to your life by accepting Him as your Lord and Savior, then your sins have been forgiven. They have also been forgotten in the sense that God will never remember them against you again (Isaiah 43:25 and Hebrews 8:12).

Think of it — forgiven and forgotten! That is grace!

The Judgment of the Just

If the Redeemed will never be judged of their sins, then what will they be judged of, and when will the judgment take place?

The Bible teaches that the Redeemed will be judged of their works, not to determine their eternal destiny, but to determine their degrees of reward.

Christians do not work to be saved; they work because they are saved. In fact, the Bible says they are saved to do good works (Ephesians 2:10 and Titus 2:14). Such good works, if properly done, will be done in the power of the Holy Spirit (1 Peter 4:11) and for the glory of God (1 Corinthians 10:31).

The Significance of Spiritual Gifts

Paul says in 1 Corinthians 12 that every person who is born again receives at least one supernatural spiritual gift from the Holy Spirit. A person may receive more than one gift. And, if you are a good steward of the gifts you receive, then you may receive additional gifts as you develop spiritually (Luke 19:26).

God expects us to use our spiritual gifts to advance His kingdom. This is what the judgment of works will be all about. Each of us who are redeemed will stand before the Lord Jesus and give an accounting of how we used our gifts to advance the kingdom of God on earth.

We will be judged as to the quantity of our works (Luke 19:11-27 and Romans 2:6-7). We will be judged as to the quality of our works (1 Corinthians 3:10-14). Finally, we will be judged as to the motivation of our works (1 Corinthians 4:5).

I can imagine some famous evangelist being brought before the Lord for judgment.

"How did you use your spiritual gifts to advance my kingdom?" asks the Lord.

"I used my gifts as a teacher and evangelist to preach the gospel to millions," replies the preacher.

"Yes," says the Lord, "you certainly did that. But, I know your heart, and thus I know your motivation. You preached not because you loved Me but because you wanted to become famous. You wanted to have your picture published on the cover of *Time* magazine. You accomplished that in February of 1953. Here's your picture. That's all the reward I have for you!"

And then I can imagine the Lord calling up a little old lady that no one has ever heard of.

"Dear, on the day you accepted Me as your Lord and Savior, I gave you one gift — the gift of mercy. And every time someone was ill, you were the first to offer comfort and encouragement. You were the one who organized the prayer chain. Every time someone went to the hospital, you were the first to visit them. Every time someone died, you were the one who organized the meals. And you did all of these things simply because you loved Me."

The Lord will give her a crown full of so many jewels that she will have a neck ache for eternity!

Seriously, there will be degrees of rewards. They will be manifested in the crowns we receive (2 Timothy 4:7-8), the robes we wear (Revelation 19:8), and the degrees of ruling authority which we exercise with the Lord (Luke 19:11-27).

The Timing of the Judgments

When and where will the judgment of the Redeemed take place? The Bible indicates the judgment of believers who have lived and died during the Church Age will occur in Heaven before the judgment seat of Jesus, immediately following the Rapture of the Church (2 Corinthians 5:10 and Revelation 19:6-9).

Those who are saved and martyred during the Tribulation will be judged at the end of that period when they are resurrected at the Second Coming of Christ (Revelation 20:4). The Tribulation saints who live to the end of that terrible period are another group that will be judged at the Second Coming of Jesus in "the sheep and goat judgment" portrayed in Matthew 25:31-46. The Old Testament saints will also be judged at the time of the Second Coming (Ezekiel 20:34-38).

The Confidence of the Just

Those who accept Jesus as Lord and Savior in this life and who remain faithful to Him can face their eternal judgment with confidence.

The Apostle John asserted this glorious fact when he stated that those who abide in the love of Christ "may have confidence in the day of judgment" (1John 4:17). He further emphasized this point with these words: "These things I have written to you who believe in the name of the Son of God, so that you may know that you have eternal life" (1 John 5:13).

King David had asserted this confidence long before in Psalm 32, and Paul quoted it in his letter to the Romans:

> Blessed are those whose lawless deeds have
>   been forgiven,
> And whose sins have been covered.
> Blessed is the man whose sin the Lord will
>   not take into account. (Romans 4:7-8)

If you have accepted Jesus as your Lord and Savior, and you are still harboring any doubt as to your eternal destiny, it is because you are trusting in your own works rather than relying on the grace of God.

I lived with such doubts for years because I grew up in a works-salvation church. I lived a spiritually schizophrenic life, never knowing for sure whether I was saved or lost. I would have confidence one moment and be drowning in doubt the next moment.

I never heard any preaching about grace. After 30 years of faithful church attendance, if you had asked me about grace, I would have thought you were talking about some woman by that name!

I will never forget the day when I discovered the verse that steered me toward the grace of God. It was Romans 8:1 which says, "Therefore there is now no condemnation for those who are in Christ Jesus."

My next discovery was equally thrilling. It was the Apostle John's statement in 1 John 1:7 — "If we walk in the Light as He Himself is in the Light, we have fellowship with one another, and the blood of Jesus His Son cleanses us from all sin." I call that a "Hallelujah! verse."

An Illustration of God's Grace

Each morning my wife and I begin our day with a devotional time together. We read from the Bible and from a devotional book and then pray together.

Several years ago, we ran across a devotional that was so powerful that I pledged then and there that I would share it with as many people as possible until my death or the Lord's return, whichever came first. It contained a vivid illustration of the grace of God as expressed in the sacrifice of His Son. I have since misplaced the devotional book it came out of, so I cannot give credit to the one who wrote the illustration. His or her credit will have to come from the Lord. Let me share it with you.

Back in the Gold Rush days of the 1840's and 50's thousands of people made the long trek across our nation from the East coast to the West in wagon trains, following a variety of routes.

There were many things the wagon masters feared, such as arriving at water holes that had dried up or become polluted. Other dangers included wind and hail storms, plagues, blizzards, and Indian attacks.

One of the most fearsome things was the prairie fire, particularly since they often traveled at the rate of 40 to 50 miles an hour, depending on the strength of the winds and the dryness of the grass. Yet, as much of a danger as these fires presented, there is no record of any wagon train ever being lost to one of them.

The reason is that there was an ingenious way of protecting a wagon train from such a threat. When the wagon master would spot smoke on the horizon, he would immediately halt the wagon train and light the grass on the side of the train away from the fire. Once the grass had burned away sufficiently, he would circle the wagons in the burned out area, take off their cloth tops, and wait for the fire.

When the fire arrived, it would simply burn around the wagons and move on without causing any damage.

Now, this is an illustration of what happened to Jesus as He hung on the Cross. All the sins that you and I have ever committed, and ever will commit, were placed upon Him, and the wrath of God was poured out upon Him. He took the wrath that we deserve.

When you accept Jesus as your Lord and Savior, you step into the area where the wrath of God has already been poured out — where the fire has already fallen — and you become immune from God's wrath.

That is the reason that the Apostle Paul wrote these words about those who have put their faith in Jesus: "For God has not destined us for wrath, but for obtaining salvation though our Lord Jesus Christ" (1 Thessalonians 5:9).

The Judgment of the Unjust

Let's turn our attention now to the unjust, to those who die outside a faith relationship with God. All the unrighteous who have ever lived will be resurrected and judged at the end of the millennial reign of Jesus.

The terrible judgment of the unrighteous is pictured in Revelation 20:11-15. It is called the "Great White Throne Judgment."

We are told that the wicked also will be judged of their works. But their judgment will be radically different from the judgment of the Redeemed. Whereas the Redeemed are judged of their works to determine their degrees of reward, the lost are judged of their works to determine their eternal destiny.

And since no one can be justified before God by their works (Isaiah 64:6 and Ephesians 2:8-10), all will be condemned to Hell. That's why I call this judgment "the judgment of the damned."

The unjust are also judged for another reason. There are going to be degrees of punishment (Luke 12:35-48 and 20: 45-47).

There is a popular myth in Christendom that says, "All sin is equal in the eyes of God." That is not true. The only way in which all sin is equal is that any sin, whether a white lie or murder, condemns us before God and necessitates a Savior.

But all sin is not equal in the eyes of God. For example, Proverbs 6:16-19 lists seven sins that the Lord particularly hates, including "hands that shed innocent blood." And the Bible makes it very clear that idolatry is a sin that is especially heinous in the eyes of God (Exodus 20:3-5).

Because God considers some sins worse than others, there will be degrees of punishment (Revelation 22:12), and these degrees will be specified at the Great White Throne judgment.

A Call to Repentance

Where do you stand with respect to the inevitable judgment which you will face before the Lord?

If you are a Christian, do you know what spiritual gifts you have been given? Are you using them to advance the Lord's kingdom? Is your motivation a love of the Lord?

If you have never confessed Jesus as your Lord and Savior, do you really want to participate in the judgment of the damned? Do you realize that the Bible says, "Every knee shall bow and every tongue confess that Jesus is Lord"? That means Mao Tse-tung and every vile person like him who has ever lived will one day make the confession of Jesus' lordship. You will too.

I urge you to make that confession now so that you can participate in the resurrection and judgment of the righteous. As you consider your decision, weigh carefully the following words from the book of Hebrews:

> Christ also, having been offered once to bear
> the sins of many, shall appear a second time
> for salvation without reference to sin, to those
> who eagerly await Him. — Hebrews 9:28

Notice carefully that this verse promises that for those who are ready for Him, Jesus will come "without reference to sin." That is a wonderful promise.

Questions and Answers

1) When you speak of resurrection, are you talking about the resurrection of our bodies or our spirits?

When the Bible speaks of resurrection, it is always talking about the resurrection of the body. The spirit needs no resurrection since it continues to consciously exist after death. It is the body that ceases to have animation, and it is the body that needs to be re-animated.

The idea that our current physical existence will be replaced in eternity by a purely spiritual form of life is foreign to the Scriptures. It is a concept of both Greek philosophy and Eastern religions, but not the Bible.

God is determined to redeem all of His creation — and that includes the plant and animal kingdoms and the heavens and the earth, all of which have been polluted by Man's sin. All will be restored to their original perfection to the honor and glory of God.

The book of Revelation reveals that when the Eternal State begins, God will "make all things new" (Revelation 21:5). Notice, it does not say He will make new things. Rather, He is going to refresh, redeem and make perfect His original creation.

I love the way the psalmist describes the process poetically in Psalm 102. He states that even though the heavens and the earth will "wear out like a garment," the Lord will change them "like clothing" (Psalm 102:26).

2) What about other resurrections? You mention the resurrection of Jesus and the resurrections that will occur at the Rapture, the Second Coming of Jesus and the end of the Millennium, but what about the other resurrections mentioned in the Bible? Consider, for example, the resurrections of Lazarus, Eutychus and Dorcas. Where do these fit into the sequence of resurrections you outline?

With the exception of Jesus' resurrection, I focused on resurrections that are yet to occur in the end times. It is true that there are stories in the Bible about other people who came back from the dead, but these are not related to the resurrections of the end times.

But these stories are worth our consideration, for they will help us better understand the true meaning of resurrection. Here is a list of persons brought back from the dead, recorded in both the Old and New Testaments:

1) The widow's son by Elijah (1 Kings 17:17-24).

2) The Shunammite's son by Elisha (2 Kings 4:18-37).

3) A man whose body was placed in Elisha's tomb (2 Kings 13:20-21).

4) The daughter of Jairus by Jesus (Mark 5:21-24, 35-43).

5) The widow's son in Nain by Jesus (Luke 7:11-15).

6) Lazarus by Jesus (John 11:30-44).

7) A number of saints in Jerusalem at the time of Jesus' death and resurrection (Matthew 27:50-53).

8) Tabitha (Dorcas) by Peter (Acts 9:36-43).

9) Eutychus by Paul (Acts 20:7-12).

It is interesting that the Bible never refers to any of these people as having been resurrected. Instead, it uses other terminology to describe what happened to them:

1) The widow's son: "the life of the child returned to him and he revived" (1 Kings 17:22).

2) The Shunammite's son: "the flesh of the child became warm . . . and the lad opened his eyes" (2 Kings 4:34-35).

3) The man thrown into Elisha's tomb: "he revived and stood on his feet" (2 Kings 13:21).

4) The daughter of Jairus: "the girl rose and began to walk" (Mark 5:42).

5) The widow's son in Nain: "the dead man sat up and began to speak" (Luke 7:15).

6) Lazarus: "He who had died came forth" (John 11:44).

7) Many dead saints in Jerusalem: "saints who had fallen asleep were raised" (Matthew 27:52).

8) Tabitha (Dorcas): "she opened her eyes and . . . sat up" (Acts 9:40).

9) Eutychus: "and they took the boy away alive" (Acts 20:12).

The reason there is no mention of resurrection in any of these cases is because these people were not resurrected. They were, instead, resuscitated. In other words, they were re-animated to die again at a later time. True resurrection in the biblical sense is resurrection to eternal life.

That is the reason that Jesus is referred to by Paul as the "first fruits" of the resurrection (1 Corinthians 15:23). Jesus was the first person to experience resurrection from the dead to eternal life.

In Hebrews 11:35 there is a reference to the two Old Testament stories of sons of widows being resuscitated. In the New American Standard Bible the passage reads: "Women received back their dead by resurrection . . ." This is an unfortunate translation. It is more properly translated in the KJV, the NKJV and the NIV as, "Women received their dead raised to life again . . ." The key Greek work used in this passage is *anastasis*, which mean a "raising or rising up," as from a seat or from the dead.

There is another resurrection of the dead that is mentioned in the Scriptures that most likely is a true resurrection. It is an event that the Bible prophesies will occur in the middle of the Great Tribulation when God removes His supernatural protection from His two special witnesses in Jerusalem and allows the Antichrist to kill them (Revelation 11:3-7).

We are told that their bodies will lie in the streets of Jerusalem for three and a half days, at which time, with all the world observing, "the breath of God" will come into them, they will stand on their feet, and they will be taken up into heaven in a cloud (Revelation 11:11-12). This appears to be a true resurrection and would thus have to be considered another of the stages in the "first resurrection" of the righteous.

3) Was the concept of resurrection to eternal life known to Old Testament saints? Or, is it a New Testament revelation?

The concept is not prominent in the Old Testament, but there are certainly passages that teach bodily resurrection to eternal life.

Many scholars believe that Job is the oldest book in the Bible, written before the Pentateuch (the first five books of Moses). In this ancient book, there are two places where the concept of resurrection is affirmed.

The first is when Job answers a question that he asks himself: "If a man dies, will he live again?" (Job 14:14). This evidently was a rhetorical question asked to provoke thought rather than to elicit an answer, because Job immediately answered it by observing, "All the days of my struggle I will wait, until my change comes. You will call, and I will answer You . . ." (Job 14:14-15).

Later, Job once again affirmed his Holy Spirit inspired belief in resurrection when he made a bold proclamation (Job 19:25-27):

> And as for me, I know that my Redeemer lives,
> And at the last, He will take His stand on the earth.
> Even after my skin is destroyed,
> Yet from my flesh I shall see God;
> Whom I myself shall behold,
> And whom my eyes shall see and not another.
> My heart faints within me.

What an incredible statement at the very dawn of history, before any written Scriptures! Read it again, slowly, and meditate upon it.

Job is saying that he is confident that in the end times his Redeemer will come to this earth and revive Job's flesh so that he will see God with his own eyes. It is a revelation so glorious that Job concludes by saying that the very thought of it is enough to cause him to faint!

Like Job, King David of Judah also affirmed confidence in his own resurrection in Psalm 16:10 where he wrote, "You will not abandon my soul to Sheol." Sheol is the Hebrew word for what the New Testament calls Hades in the Greek language. At David's time it was the temporary holding place for the spirits of the dead. Continuing in that same verse, David prophesied that the Messiah would be resurrected: "Nor will You allow Your Holy One to undergo decay."

In the following psalm, David again affirmed his faith in his personal resurrection when he wrote, "As for me, I shall behold Your face in righteousness; I will be satisfied with Your likeness when I awake" (Psalm 17:15). And David continued this theme in his most famous psalm: "Surely, goodness and lovingkindness will follow me all the days of my life, and I will dwell in the house of the Lord forever" (Psalm 23:6).

There are other references to resurrection in the Psalms (Psalm 49:15 and Psalm 73:24), and there are references in Isaiah. For example, in Isaiah 25:8 the prophet stated that a time will come when God "will swallow up death for all time, and the Lord God will wipe tears away from all faces." And in the next chapter, Isaiah wrote (Isaiah 26:19):

> Your dead will live;
> Their corpses will rise.
> You who lie in the dust, awake and shout for joy,
> For your dew is as the dew of the dawn,
> And the earth will give birth to the departed spirits.

Perhaps the two best known references in the Hebrew Scriptures to resurrection are found in Hosea and Daniel. Hosea presented rhetorical questions asked by God: "Shall I ransom them [the dead] from the power of Sheol? Shall I redeem them from death?" (Hosea 13:14). Hosea then recorded God's answer to these questions: "O Death, where are your thorns? O Sheol, where is your sting?" Paul quoted this verse in 1 Corinthians 15:55 where he used it to affirm the resurrection of the saints.

The passage in Daniel is one of the most explicit ones in the Old Testament about resurrection. He prophesied that in the end times "there will be a time of distress" that will be unparalleled in Jewish history. This is a reference to the Great Tribulation, the time of "Jacob's trouble" (Jeremiah 30:7 — NKJV). Daniel then said that at the end of that terrible period, "many of those who sleep in the dust of the ground will awake," some "to everlasting life, but the others to disgrace and everlasting contempt" (Daniel 12:2).

Despite these references to a future resurrection, the Jewish religious leaders in the First Century, called Sadducees and Pharisees, were sharply divided over the issue of resurrection. The Pharisees believed in resurrection; the Sadducees did not. This difference in theology was rooted in the fact that the Sadducees gave priority to the writings of Moses (the Pentateuch). They thus argued that since Moses made no reference to a future resurrection, there was no basis for believing in one.

The Apostle Paul manipulated this difference to his advantage when he was brought before the Sanhedrin Council to be tried for heresy. Knowing that the Council was composed of both Sadducees and Pharisees, he proclaimed: "I am a Pharisee, a son of Pharisees; I am on trial for the hope and resurrection of the dead!" (Acts 23:6). The Council members then turned on each other and a great uproar occurred (Acts 23:7-10).

With regard to the Sadducees' denial that Moses ever mentioned resurrection, I think it is interesting that when Jesus confronted them about their erroneous belief, He affirmed resurrection by quoting a passage from the writings of Moses (Mark 12:26-27):

> But regarding the fact that the dead rise again, have you not read in the book of Moses, in the passage about the burning bush, how God spoke to him, saying, "I am the God of Abraham, and the God of Isaac, and the God of Jacob"? He is

not the God of the dead, but of the living; you
are greatly mistaken.

**4) You keep quoting the verse in Hebrews 9:27 that says:
". . . it is appointed for men to die once and after this
comes judgment." What about Enoch and Elijah? Neither
one died. How do you explain this contradiction?**

The statement in Hebrews is a general principle. Enoch
and Elijah are exceptions to that principle. God is sovereign,
and He can make exceptions as He sees fit. Further exceptions would be those in the Bible who were resuscitated from
death, only to die a second time.

Incidentally, Enoch and Elijah might not be exceptions to
the general rule. I say that because I believe they are going to
be the two great witnesses of God during the first half of the
Tribulation, and those two witnesses are going to be killed by
the Antichrist (Revelation 11:7). If that is the case, then their
deaths have simply been delayed.

Many people believe the two witnesses are going to be
Elijah and Moses because they perform miracles that are
associated with these two men. But all the early Church
Fathers believed the two witnesses would be Enoch and
Elijah, and that makes sense to me since neither died and
since one is a Gentile (Enoch) and the other is a Jew. Thus, as
the two witnesses of God during the Tribulation, one would
be a spokesman to the Gentile world and the other to the
Jews.

There is another exception to the general principle that all
must die and then face judgment. I have in mind those saints
who are alive at the time of the Rapture of the Church (1
Thessalonians 4:13-18). We are told that they will be taken
up to meet the Lord in the sky, and that en route, they will be
translated from mortal to immortal. That means there is a
whole generation of Christians who will not taste death.

5) You say that as a believer I will be judged as to how I use my spiritual gifts to serve the Lord. How can I determine my spiritual gifts?

This is a very important question. I grew up in a church that taught that spiritual gifts ended in the First Century when the last apostle died. That is an unbiblical theology called Cessationism.

To the contrary, Paul taught in 1 Corinthians 1:7 that the Church will not be lacking in any spiritual gift while it awaits the return of Jesus. We are still waiting for that return, so the spiritual gifts revealed in the New Testament are still active.

As you attempt to determine your gift or gifts, keep in mind that a spiritual gift is different from a natural talent. When you are born again and you receive the indwelling presence of the Holy Spirit (Acts 2:38), you may be gifted by the Spirit where you are talented, and you may not. That explains why some very talented teachers are not gifted in teaching the Scriptures, or why some very talented singers are not gifted to lead in worship.

When I first yielded to the Lord's call on my life to serve Him full time in ministry, I knew almost nothing about spiritual gifts. I just assumed that God wanted me to be a pastor.

I discovered very quickly that I did not have the spiritual gifts to be a pastor. Effective pastors must have supernatural love, patience and compassion. They must be willing to preach Sunday after Sunday, witness little, if any, observable change in those they are preaching to, and still love them anyway.

In contrast, my gifting is prophetic in nature, meaning that I am motivated to grab a person by his lapels, shake him until his teeth rattle, and demand that he get with the program!

You will never be able to serve the Lord effectively until you determine your spiritual gifts and then begin to utilize them. Here are some guidelines for determining your spiritual gifts:

1) Pray for the Lord to reveal your gifts to you.

2) Acquaint yourself with the gifts of the Spirit. To do this you must spend some time reading and thinking about the passages that identify the gifts. See: Romans 12:3-8; 1 Corinthians 12:27-31; 1 Corinthians 14:1-19; Ephesians 4:11-13; and 1 Peter 4:7-11.

3) Take a spiritual gifts inventory exam. You can find these on the Internet. Just use a search engine and type in the phrase, "spiritual gifts inventory tests." Some of these you can take online and get instant results. For others you have to print out the test, take it, and then calculate the results. None of the tests are perfect, but they will help point you in the right direction.

4) Ask your Christian friends and pastor to help you identify your gifts. They can often help you to see the obvious that you may be blind to.

5) Read a balanced book about spiritual gifts. The best one I can recommend is *19 Gifts of the Spirit* by Leslie B. Flynn.[1]

Regarding the fourth point above, I am reminded of a humorous incident that occurred many years ago when I was teaching a class on the gifts of the Spirit. I announced that at the last session we would give each person an opportunity to identify their gifts. Each did so until we got to a fellow named Jim.

Jim said, "I'm sorry, but I think the Lord overlooked me when He was handing out gifts!"

We got a good laugh out of that remark, but everyone of us in the group knew that Jim had not been overlooked. All of us knew what spiritual gift he had been given.

One of the ladies in the group asked, "Jim, when we have a church work day on Saturdays, who is always the first to arrive?"

"Well," said Jim, "I guess it's always me."

"That's right. And who is the one who always volunteers to do all the dirty jobs no one else wants to do?"

"Well, again, I guess that's me."

"Yes, and who is the last one to always go home, usually an hour or two after everyone else has left?"

"That's me also."

"Yes, Jim, and the reason is that you have been given the supernatural gift of helps" (1 Corinthians 12:28).

Jim was delighted to discover that he really did have a spiritual gift and that he was using it mightily to help advance the Lord's kingdom. In fact, no church or ministry could exist for long without people with this seemingly unimportant but very significant gift.

One final point. Remember that gifts of the Spirit are just that — they are gifts. They are not something you have earned. No pride should ever be taken in them. Remember too that what is more important is the fruit of the Spirit: love, joy, peace, patience, kindness, goodness, faithfulness, gentleness, and self-control (Galatians 5:22-23).

6) What are some of the rewards that will be given to believers at the time of their judgment?

One will be degrees of participation in the millennial reign of Jesus (Luke 19:11-27). During those glorious thousand years, Jesus will reign as King of kings from Jerusalem (Revelation 19:16). David in his glorified body will reign as king of Israel (Ezekiel 34:23-24). Believers in their glorified bodies will be scattered across the earth to help administer the worldwide government of Jesus.

Some of us will serve as executives — presidents, kings, prime ministers, governors and mayors. Others will serve as judges. Most will be teachers. The point is that every person in a position of governing responsibility will be a person in a glorified body submitted to the guidance of the Holy Spirit (Daniel 7:18 & 27 and Revelation 2:26). It is no wonder that the earth will be filled with peace, righteousness, and justice.

One role that none of us will fill is that of legislator. There will be no abominations like the Texas Legislature or the United States Congress because all laws will be dictated by Jesus. His reign will be a theocratic one in which God's Word will serve as the constitution and the law (Psalm 2:9 and Revelation 2:27).

Many other rewards are mentioned in the Scriptures. The Rapture itself is mentioned as a "prize" for Church Age saints for it will deliver us from the horrors of the Great Tribulation (Philippians 3:14).

After the resurrection of the saved (whether it be with the Church Age saints at the Rapture or with the Old Testament saints and Tribulation martyrs at the Second Coming), we will receive special rewards in Heaven as Jesus presents us to His Father.

Each of us will be confessed by Jesus before the Father and His angels (Matthew 10:32 and Revelation 3:5). We will be honored by the Father (John 12:26), and we will be adopted as His children (Romans 8:23). We will receive glorified bodies (1 Corinthians 15:35-53), and our souls will be conformed to the image of Jesus (Romans 8:29-30). We will be given power over the "second death" (Revelation 2:11) by being granted the gift of eternal life (John 3:14-17).

Many different types of rewards will be handed out when we are judged by Jesus. Some will be granted to all. Others will be specialized rewards given for service in the kingdom. Those given to all will include such things as a new name (Revelation 2:17) and understanding of God's mysteries (1 Corinthians 13:12).[2]

Some of the specialized awards that are mentioned include the following:

1) Comfort for those who mourned (Matthew 5:4).

2) Satisfaction for those who hungered and thirsted for righteousness (Matthew 5:6).

3) Mercy for those who were merciful (Matthew 5:7).

4) Praise, honor and glory for those who were persecuted for the sake of righteousness (Matthew 5:10-12 and 1 Peter 1:6-7).

5) For those who were sacrificial, they will receive back a hundred times more than what they surrendered for Christ (Matthew 19:29).

6) Exaltation for those who were humble (Matthew 18:4).

7) Special blessings for those who rendered special service to the Church (2 Timothy 1:16-18).

8) An imperishable wreath for those who exercised self-control (1 Corinthians 9:24-27).

9) A crown of exaltation for those who were soul winners (1 Thessalonians 2:19-20).

10) A crown of righteousness for those who loved the Lord's appearing (2 Timothy 4:8).

11) A crown of life for those who endured trials (James 1:12).

12) An unfading crown of glory for those who served as elders and pastors (1 Peter 5:1-4).

13) Robes of fine linen reflecting righteous deeds (Revelation 19:8).

I think you can see now why Paul wrote that "the sufferings of this present time are not worthy to be compared with the glory that is to be revealed to us" (Romans 8:18).

Unfortunately, some will receive no special rewards beyond the reward of eternal life (1 Corinthians 3:10-15). In fact, they will suffer embarrassment at the judgment seat of Jesus when their lack of use of their spiritual gifts is revealed and they end up having nothing to put at the feet of Jesus to glorify Him (Revelation 4:10).

7) You mention the judgments of Church Age saints, Old Testament saints, Tribulation saints, and Tribulation martyrs. What about those born during the Millennium? When will they be judged?

Those born during the Millennium who never respond to Jesus in faith will be judged at the Great White Throne Judgment depicted in Revelation 20:11-15. This judgment will be held at the end of the Millennium, after Satan's last revolt has ended. It is the judgment of every person who has ever lived and died outside a faith relationship with God.

The Bible does not reveal the judgment of those who are born and saved during the Millennium. All we know for sure is that the Bible says every person will face judgment, therefore the Millennial saints will most likely be judged at the end of the Millennium, either before or after the Great White Throne Judgment.

8) In addition to the judgment of individuals, doesn't the Bible teach that God will also judge nations?

Yes. There are many passages of Scripture which teach

that God will pour out His wrath in judgment upon nations during the Great Tribulation.

Isaiah 2:14 speaks of the Lord chastising prideful "mountains and hills," which are symbols in prophetic literature of nations. Isaiah 34:2 says that the "Lord's indignation is against all the nations." Jeremiah says the Lord will "roar from on high" because He "has a controversy with the nations" (Jeremiah 25:31).

Habakkuk says the Lord will trample the nations (Habakkuk 3:12). The entire book of Zephaniah is devoted to a description of the wrath God will pour out upon the nations. God proclaims through the prophet: "All the earth will be devoured by the fire of My zeal" (Zephaniah 3:8b). Haggai says the Lord will "shake all the nations" (Haggai 2:7).

The Great Tribulation will be a special time of judgment for Israel. The wrath of God, Satan, and Man will be focused upon the Jews. Two-thirds of the Jewish people will perish in a holocaust greater than the one inflicted by the Nazis (Zechariah 13:8).

Jeremiah calls it "the time of Jacob's trouble" (Jeremiah 30:7 — KJV). Daniel refers to it as "a time of distress" unparalleled in history (Daniel 12:1). Zephaniah says the Lord's wrath will be focused in particular upon the Jews who are involved in any sort of idolatry (Zephaniah 1:4-6).

Ezekiel, Zechariah and Malachi compare the Lord's wrath against Israel to the smelting of silver and gold (Ezekiel 22:17-22 and Malachi 3:2-4), the purpose being to purify the nation by hammering them to the point where they will repent, turn their hearts to God, and receive Jesus as their Messiah (Zechariah 12:10). Here's how Zechariah puts it in Zechariah 13:9 —

> And I will bring the third part through the fire,
> Refine them as silver is refined,

And test them as gold is tested.
They will call on My name,
And I will answer them;
I will say, "They are My people,"
And they will say, "The Lord is my God."

The image of a smelting pot as a purifier is a good one because the Bible makes it clear that the fundamental purpose of the pouring out of God's judgment is to bring a remnant of the Jews to repentance so that they can be saved. This is what Paul refers to in Romans 11:26 when he speaks of "all Israel" being saved in the end times. He is speaking of those Jews still alive at the end of the Tribulation, as he makes clear in Romans 9:27 when he points out that it is a "remnant" that will be saved.

In fact, even the judgment of God upon the Gentile nations will be for the same purpose — to motivate repentance so that more people can be saved. Isn't that astonishing? Think of it — even when God pours out His wrath in judgment, His fundamental purpose is not to punish but to humble people to repentance so that they might be saved. It's what might be called God's tough love. Here's how Isaiah put it in Isaiah 26:9b — "For when the earth experiences Your judgments, the inhabitants of the world learn righteousness."

Heaven

A Song by Randy Estep

Just imagine Heaven
And what God's kingdom will be like.
Where we will live forever
With no more pain or tears or strife.
Some folks think of Heaven
As just a distant dream beyond some star,
But if it's as real as Jesus promised,
It's just as near to us as our own heart.

Just imagine living in God's New Jerusalem,
And our wandering days are over
And our weary hearts at rest in Him.
We'll wake up from our dreaming
And we'll meet our Savior face to face.
As He receives us as His children,
He will smile and say,
"Welcome home to stay."

Refrain:

Some call it "Canaan Land."
Some call it "Beulah Land."
It's called "peace beyond the river,"
A place not made with hands.
And it's that great celestial city
With mansions 'round God's throne.
But for all who know my Lord,
They call it "home."

Chapter 3

What Will Heaven Be Like?

"For here we do not have a lasting city, but we are seeking the city which is to come." — Hebrews 13:14

For many years I had little desire to go to Heaven. My only interest in Heaven was prompted by a desire to avoid Hell.

My apathy was rooted in what I had been taught about Heaven. Basically, I had been led to believe that going to Heaven meant being a disembodied spirit residing in an ethereal world, floating around on a cloud playing a harp. I just couldn't get excited about that picture!

My interest in Heaven developed slowly over a long period of time. It became a passion, in part because of my study of prophecy, but mainly because of my growing relationship with the Lord.

The more I came to know Him, the more I desired to be with Him.

A Heavenly Surprise

The reason my study of prophecy did not play the key role in developing my interest in Heaven is because the Bible is strangely silent about the subject. The Bible tells us in great detail what the Millennium will be like, but it gives us almost no detailed information about the Eternal State.

What it does tell us often comes as a great surprise to most Christians because the scriptures about Heaven have been so terribly spiritualized. For example, the Bible plainly says the Redeemed will spend eternity on a new earth, not in an ethereal place called Heaven.

Isaiah was the first to speak of this truth when he spoke of "the new heavens and the new earth" which will endure forever before the Lord (Isaiah 66:22). This truth is repeated in the book of Revelation where the apostle John says he was shown a new earth, "for the first heaven and the first earth passed away" (Revelation 21:1).

John goes on to describe the new Jerusalem descending to the new earth, "coming down out of heaven from God" (Revelation 21:2). And then he states that God Himself will come to live on the new earth (Revelation 21:3):

> Behold, the tabernacle of God is among men, and He shall dwell among them, and they shall be His people, and God Himself shall be among them.

This truth had already been revealed to the Old Testament prophets. While being taken on a prophetic tour of the millennial temple, Ezekiel was told by his guide (the Lord Jesus in a pre-incarnate appearance): "Son of man, this is the place of My throne and the place of the soles of My feet, where I will dwell among the sons of Israel forever" (Ezekiel 43:7).

The Redeemed are going to dwell forever in new bodies on a new earth in a new Jerusalem in the presence of Almighty God and His Son, Jesus. Heaven will come to earth!

Two Heavens

The fact that Heaven is coming to earth is one of the reasons there is so much confusion about Heaven. When most Christians think about Heaven, they think of an ethereal world that exists far away someplace in outer space. But the Heaven that exists now is not the same as the Heaven where the Redeemed are going to live eternally.

The current Heaven where God resides (1 Kings 8:30) was created by God (Revelation 10:6). It is a "high and holy place" (Isaiah 57:15) that is located in "the third heaven" (2 Corinthians 12:1-4). The first heaven is the atmosphere of this planet. The second heaven is outer space. The third heaven is beyond our cosmos.

God's throne room is located in Heaven (Isaiah 66:1 and Revelation 4:2). And although God is spirit (John 24:4), Heaven is a very tangible, material place. We know this because the Apostle John was taken up to Heaven and given a tour which he describes in Revelation 4 and 5.

John's Description of Heaven

John described God's throne as having the appearance of an emerald surrounded by a rainbow and emitting brilliant light (Revelation 4:1-3). The throne was guarded by four mysterious "living creatures" (Revelation 4:6), and seated around the throne were 24 elders clothed in white with gold crowns (Revelation 4:4). Behind the elders were myriads of angels (Revelation 5:11), and all of these beings — the elders, the angels and the living creatures — worshiped day and night without ceasing, singing songs of praise and adoration (Revelation 4:8, 11 and Revelation 5:9-10, 12-13).

John saw Jesus in Heaven (Revelation 5:5-10) where He is serving as our high priest at His Father's throne (Hebrews 9:11-15), interceding for us as the mediator of our prayers (1 Timothy 2:5). He also saw the spirits of dead saints clothed in white robes (Revelation 7:9) standing around God's throne. In addition to worshiping God, the saints are portrayed as serving Him day and night (Revelation 7:15).

Other Descriptions of Heaven

The Apostle John is not the only person who has been given a glimpse of Heaven and God's throne room. The first to be mentioned in the Scriptures is Moses. While leading the children of Israel through the wilderness, God called him and his brother Aaron, together with Nadab, Abihu and 70 elders of the tribes to come up on Mount Sinai to commune with Him. "And they saw the God of Israel; and under His feet there appeared to be a pavement of sapphire, as clear as the sky itself" (Exodus 24:9-10).

The next person to be allowed to see God's throne room in Heaven was the oral prophet Micaiah who lived during the reign of King Jehoshaphat of Judah. During a conference with King Jehoshaphat and King Ahab of Israel, Micaiah reported, "I saw the Lord sitting on His throne, and all the host of heaven standing by Him on His right and on His left" (1 Kings 22:19).

Isaiah had a similar experience at the time of his call to be a prophet. He wrote that he "saw the Lord sitting on a throne, lofty and exalted, with the train of His robe filling the temple" (Isaiah 6:1). Special angelic creatures called Seraphim flew about God's throne crying out, "Holy, Holy, Holy, is the Lord of hosts, the whole earth is full of His glory" (Isaiah 6:3).

The prophet Ezekiel witnessed a similar scene on the day he was anointed a prophet (Ezekiel 1:1-28). His was a very spectacular experience. He saw four angelic creatures darting about in the sky, similar in appearance to the "living creatures" John saw in God's throne room (Ezekiel 1:1-10 and Revelation 4:6-8). Later, Ezekiel refers to them as Cherubim (Ezekiel 10:15). Each creature seemed to be riding on a sparkling wheel, and they "ran to and fro like bolts of lightning" (Ezekiel 1:14-21).

These creatures led Ezekiel to the throne of God. Like John, he noted that the throne had a rainbow about it, and the person sitting on the throne, "who had the appearance of a man," was surrounded by "something like fire" emitting "a radiance" (Ezekiel 1:26-28).

The prophet Daniel was the next person allowed to see God's throne room. He had "a dream and vision" (Daniel 7:1) in which he saw "the Ancient of Days" on His throne, and the "throne was ablaze with fire" (Daniel 7:9). Myriads of beings were present to serve God (Daniel 7:10). And standing before the throne, Daniel saw the Messiah which he described as "One like a Son of Man" (Daniel 7:13).

In the New Testament the first person given a glimpse of Heaven was Stephen, who is described as "a man full of faith and of the Holy Spirit" (Acts 6:5). He was arrested by the Sanhedrin Council as part of its effort to stamp out Christianity. After preaching a mighty sermon to them in which he called them "stiff-necked and uncircumcised in heart" and accused them of murdering the Messiah (Acts 7:51-52), they reacted in rage and began stoning him to death. As he was dying, "he gazed intently into heaven and saw the glory of God and Jesus standing at the right hand of God" (Acts 7:55).

The only other person the Scriptures reveal being given a glimpse of Heaven is the Apostle Paul. After his dramatic conversion on the road to Damascus (Acts 9:1-9), Paul says he "was caught up to the third heaven," which he called "Paradise" (2 Corinthians 12:1-4). Unlike the others, he does not present any description of what he saw. He simply states that he heard "inexpressible words which a man is not permitted to speak" (2 Corinthians 12:4).

So, to summarize, the current Heaven is located in the "third heaven." It contains the throne room of God the Father. Jesus is present there, as are the spirits of dead saints and myriads of angels. It is a place of never ending worship.

Satan's Access to Heaven

One final thing about the current Heaven that should be noted is that Satan has access to it. The book of Job pictures Satan before God's throne requesting permission to test Job (Job 1:6-12). The book of Revelation says that Satan is an "accuser of the brethren" and that he "accuses them before our God day and night" (Revelation 12:10).

But Revelation reveals that a day is coming when that nefarious activity will cease. It says that in the middle of the Great Tribulation, Satan will try one last time to take God's throne. He will battle the Archangel Michael and his angels, and he will be defeated (Revelation 12:7-9). Satan will be cast down to earth, and his access to Heaven will be cut off (Revelation 12:10-11). He will know then that his time is short, and he will proceed to try to kill every Jew on earth (Revelation 12:12-17).

The Future Change in Heaven

This Heaven where God now resides is going to come to earth after the millennial reign of Jesus has ended and the current earth has been refreshed and redeemed through fire, producing the new earth of eternity. Revelation says that we will be lowered down to that new earth inside our eternal city, the new Jerusalem (Revelation 21:2, 10-11). And Revelation 21:3 says that God will come down to the new earth and tabernacle among His people.

The throne room of God will be moved from the third heaven to the new earth. Since Heaven is where God resides, Heaven will come to earth. Therefore, when Christians speak of living eternally in Heaven, what they are really saying is that they will live forever on this earth, redeemed and returned to its original perfection.

The New Earth

To better understand the new earth that will be the eternal abode of the Redeemed, it is necessary to take a look at the five earths that are revealed in the Scriptures. Most people are surprised to learn that the Bible reveals that we are currently living on earth number three and that there are two earths yet to come.

Earth 1

The first earth was the one created in the beginning (Genesis 1:1). It was perfect in every respect (Genesis 1:31). But because of Man's sin, God placed a curse upon the earth (Genesis 3:17-19).

Have you ever stopped to think what a "perfect" earth must have been like? There certainly were no meat-eating animals or poisonous animals or poisonous plants. All of nature was at peace with itself and with Man. Adam and Eve did not have to strive against nature in order to produce their food. And there were no natural cataclysms like tornados, hurricanes, tsunamis, and earthquakes.

The Bible indicates that the curse radically altered the nature of God's original creation. Instead of Man exercising dominion over nature, as originally planned (Genesis 1:26, 28), nature rose up in conflict with Man, as poisonous plants, carnivorous animals and climatic cataclysms suddenly appeared.

Earth 2

The curse radically altered the original earth, but the second earth was still quite different from the one we live on today. There is much biblical evidence in both Genesis and Job that the second earth had a thick vapor canopy which shielded life from the ultraviolet radiation of the sun, contributing to the long life spans recorded in Genesis (see Genesis 2:5-6 and Job 38:8-11).

The whole earth was like a greenhouse with thick vegetation growing everywhere, even at the poles. There was also probably only one large land mass.

Once again the sinful rebellion of Mankind motivated God to change the nature of the earth (Genesis 6:11-13). The change agent this time was water. It appears that God caused the vapor canopy to collapse (Genesis 7:11). He also caused "fountains of the great deep" to break forth upon the surface of the earth (Genesis 7:11).

Earth 3

Like the curse, the flood radically altered the nature of the earth. It produced the third earth, the earth we live on now.

The earth tilted on its axis, forming the polar caps. The unified land mass was split apart, forming the continents as we now know them (which is why they fit together like a jigsaw puzzle — see Genesis 10:25). And the vapor canopy was so completely depleted that ultraviolet radiation began to reach the earth in unprecedented levels, resulting in greatly reduced life spans, first to 120 years and then to 70 years.

The Bible reveals that the current earth will be radically changed again at the Second Advent of Jesus. The change agents will be earthquakes on the earth and supernatural phenomena in the heavens.

The changes produced will so totally alter the earth and its atmosphere that Isaiah refers to "the new heavens and the new earth" which will exist during the reign of the Lord (Isaiah 65:17).

Earth 4

The fourth earth — the millennial earth — will be very different from the present earth. The earthquakes that will produce it will be the most severe in history.

At the Second Coming of Jesus, every valley will be lifted, every mountain will be lowered, and every island will be moved (Revelation 6:12-14 and 16:17-21). Jerusalem will be lifted up, and Mt. Zion will become the highest of all the mountains (Zechariah 14:10 and Micah 4:1).

The vapor canopy will likely be restored because life spans will be expanded to what they were at the beginning of time (Isaiah 65:20, 22).

Further evidence that the vapor canopy will be restored is to be found in the fact that all the earth will become abundant once again with lush vegetation (Isaiah 30:23-26 and Amos 9:13-14). The Dead Sea will also become alive (Ezekiel 47: 1-9).

Most important, the curse will be partially lifted, making it possible for Man to be reconciled to nature and for nature to be reconciled to itself. The wolf will dwell with the lamb because the wolf will no longer be carnivorous. The nursing child will play with the cobra because the cobra will no longer be poisonous (Isaiah 11:8).

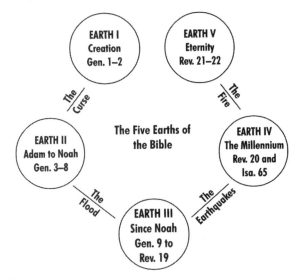

Earth 5

But Satan's last revolt at the end of the Millennium will leave the earth polluted and devastated (Revelation 20:7-9). Thus, at the end of the Lord's reign, God will take the Redeemed off the earth, place them in the New Jerusalem, and then cleanse the earth with fire (2 Peter 3:10-13).

In other words, God will superheat this earth in a fiery inferno and then reshape it like a hot ball of wax. The result will be the "new heavens and new earth" prophesied in Isaiah 66 and Revelation 21.

This will be the fifth earth, the perfected, eternal earth where the Redeemed will spend eternity in the New Jerusalem in the presence of God (Revelation 21:1-4). The curse will be completely lifted from this earth (Revelation 22:3).

The New Jerusalem

The most detailed information which the Scriptures give about Heaven pertains to our eternal abode — the new Jerusalem. Twenty verses in Chapter 21 of Revelation are devoted to a description of it.

The information contained in Revelation 21 is not the first reference in the Bible to the new Jerusalem. It is mentioned in Hebrews 11:10 as a city "whose architect and builder is God." Jesus made a reference to it that is recorded in John 14:1-4. He called it His "Father's house," and He said He would prepare a place in it for His Church.

Jesus is currently expanding, embellishing, and beautifying this house which God the Father designed and built. Jesus is preparing it for His bride, just as in Old Testament times a bridegroom would add a room onto his father's house to accommodate himself and his bride.

The city is described in Revelation as beautifully decorated, like "a bride adorned for her husband" (Revelation 21:2). Later, John actually refers to the city as the bride of the Lamb (Revelation 21:9), because the city contains the bride of Christ, His Church.

As I said before, I believe this implies that at the end of the Millennium all the Redeemed will be taken off the earth and placed in the new Jerusalem which will most likely be suspended in the heavens. From that vantage point we will watch the greatest fireworks display in all of history as the earth is cleansed and redeemed with fire, producing the new, eternal earth. Then, we will be lowered down to that new earth inside the new Jerusalem.

The city will be spectacular in both size and appearance. It will be in the form of a cube that is 1,500 miles in every direction! And it will reflect "the glory of God" (Revelation 21:11, 16).

The Size of the City

The incredible size means the city would stretch from Canada to the Gulf of Mexico and from the Atlantic coast of America to Colorado. It would also extend 1,500 miles into the atmosphere.

This tremendous extension of the city vertically into the air is a clue that the new earth may be considerably larger than the current earth. Otherwise, the city would not be proportional to its surroundings.

Would such a city be able to adequately accommodate all the Redeemed? That's a good question. The best answer I have ever run across is the one provided by Dr. Henry Morris in his book *The Revelation Record*.[1]

Dr. Morris postulates the total number of Redeemed might be as many as 20 billion. He further guesses that approximately 50 percent of the new Jerusalem might be devoted to streets, parks and public buildings. Can 20 billion people be squeezed into only half the space of this city?

The answer is yes! In fact, it can be done easily. Each person would have a cubical block with about 75 acres of surface on each face. We are talking about an immense city!

This assumes, of course, that our new glorified bodies will be immune to the current law of gravity, as are the bodies of angels. This is a safe assumption, for Philippians 3:21 says that our glorified bodies will be like the body of Jesus after

His resurrection, and His body was not subject to gravity, as evidenced by His ascension into Heaven.

This is the reason the city will be so tall. We will be able to utilize and enjoy all levels of it. There will most likely be vertical streets as well as horizontal ones.

The Beauty of the City

And what streets they will be! The Bible says they will be "pure gold, like transparent glass" (Revelation 21:21). In fact, the whole city will be made of pure gold with the appearance of clear glass (Revelation 21:18).

The city will sit on a foundation made of 12 layers of precious stones (Revelation 21:19-20). Each layer will feature the name of one of the 12 apostles (Revelation 21:14). The city will be surrounded by a jasper wall over 200 feet high (Revelation 21:17). There will be 12 gates, three on each side, and each one will be named for one of the tribes of Israel (Revelation 21:12).

And yes, the gates will be "pearly gates," each one consisting of one huge pearl (Revelation 21:21).

Best of all, God the Father and Jesus will both reside in the city with us (Revelation 21:22). The Shekinah Glory of God will illuminate the city constantly, and thus there will be no night nor will there ever be any need for any type of artificial light or the light of the sun (Revelation 22:5).

The throne of God and His Son will be in the city, and "a river of the water of life, clear as crystal" will flow down the middle of the city's main street with the tree of life growing on both sides of the river, yielding 12 kinds of fruit — a different fruit each month (Revelation 22:1-2).

That's it. God's Word only gives us a glimpse of Heaven. But what a tantalizing glimpse it is! It's a glimpse of perfect peace and joy and beauty.

The Activities of Heaven

What will we do for eternity? Again, the Word is strangely silent. All it says is that we "shall serve Him" (Revelation 22:3).[2]

I have fantasized a lot about our Heavenly activities. I can imagine us spending a great deal of our time in worship, singing the psalms of King David, with him directing us. I think it is likely that our talents will be magnified, and we will be able to sing or paint or write with a majesty and scope we never imagined possible — and all to the glory of God!

Surely we will spend considerable time in the study of God's Word. Think of studying the gospel of John with the apostle John as the teacher! I thrill to the thought of Jesus teaching the Old Testament, even as He did to His disciples following His resurrection (Luke 24:44-45). The Word of God is infinite in its depth, and I believe we will continue learning from it forever.

As we study the Word, I believe we will grow in spiritual maturity in the likeness of Jesus. And since God is infinite, no matter how much we grow in His likeness, there will just be that much more growing ahead of us. In this regard, I suspect that our spiritual growth will pick up where it left off in this life.

Sometimes, I really get far out in my thinking about Heaven. For example, I can imagine the Lord giving us the opportunity to see "instant video replays" of great events in Bible history. I hope so. I would like to see the dividing of the Red Sea, the destruction of Jericho, and the resurrection of Lazarus.

And what about tours of the universe? Surely we will be able to travel through space in our glorified bodies and see the miracles of God's creation up close. Imagine visiting all the planets in our galaxy as well as touring thousands of other galaxies!

Reigning with Jesus

But what does it mean in Revelation 22:3 where it says we will serve God as His "bond-servants"? I'm not sure. I suppose it means we will be given productive work to do. What that work will be I can't say for sure. But there is a hint in Revelation 22:5 where it says we will reign with the Lord "forever and ever."

To reign implies, of necessity, that we must reign over someone. Who will that be? Again, there is an intriguing clue. Revelation 21:24-27 refers to "nations" that will live on the new earth outside the new Jerusalem. Revelation 22:2 indicates that the people composing these nations will be in fleshly bodies, for it says that the leaves of the tree of life will be used for "the healing of the nations."

A Prophetic Mystery

Who are these "nations"? This is one of the greatest mysteries of Bible prophecy. There are as many different guesses as there are commentaries on the book of Revelation.

Could they be the Redeemed who accept Jesus during the Millennium? Nothing is said about the ultimate destiny of those who are saved during the Millennium. No promises are made to them of glorified bodies.

I don't know the answer. It is one of those areas where we look into a dimly lit mirror and will not understand fully until we stand "face to face" with the Lord (1 Corinthians 13:12).

Heavenly Fellowship

This brings me to the greatest blessing of Heaven. Revelation 22:4 says we shall see the face of God!

The Word says in Exodus 33:20 that no man has ever seen the face of God. But we will be given that privilege when we fellowship with Him in Heaven.

And that is really what Heaven is all about. We will experience an intimacy with the Lord that transcends anything possible in this life. We were created for fellowship with God (John 4:23), and that purpose will reach its zenith in the Eternal State as we live in God's presence.

That is why Paul wrote, "to live is Christ, and to die is gain" (Philippians 1:21). He went on to explain that to continue living in the flesh meant the opportunity for fruitful labor in the Lord's kingdom. But he still had a desire to depart this life, for that departure would open the door for sweet, intimate, personal fellowship with the Lord (Philippians 1:22-23).

What about you? Are you clinging to this world, or do you yearn for Heaven?

The more you come to know the Lord, the more you will love Him. And the more you love Him, the more You will desire to be with Him.

That's only natural. We always desire to be with those whom we love.

Longing for Heaven

I love my wife dearly. We have been married for more than fifty years. I have to travel a lot. I call her every night I'm on the road to tell her that I love her. I send her mushy love cards. And when I have to be gone for an extended period, I send her gifts like bouquets of flowers.

I love to talk with my wife by phone. I love to send her love notes. I love to surprise her with gifts. But none of these are substitutes for being with her! When you love someone you want to be with them.

In like manner, I love to fellowship with the Lord in worship, in Bible study, and in prayer. But these spiritual activities are no substitute for actually being with the Lord.

Because I love Him, I want to be with Him. Personal, intimate fellowship with the Lord — that is the essence of Heaven.

May it become a reality very soon!

Questions and Answers

1) Can I go to Heaven by doing good works?

The idea that people can earn their way to Heaven through good works is the most widely accepted religious belief in the world today.

It is characteristic of every religion in the world except Christianity. I recently heard Dr. Robert Jeffress, pastor of First Baptist Church in Dallas, address this issue in a novel way. He said, "Every religion in the world, except Christianity, can be spelled DO. Christianity alone can be spelled DONE!"

What he meant by that insightful statement is that all the religions of the world, except Christianity, require you to compile a record of good deeds in order to be saved. In contrast, Christianity says that Jesus did everything needed for our salvation on the Cross when He died for us, which is why His last words were, "It is finished" (John 19:30).

From the beginning of the Bible to its end, we are taught over and over that we cannot be saved by our good works. The prophet Isaiah stated this truth dramatically when he wrote that "all our righteous deeds are like a filthy garment" (Isaiah 64:6). In the New Testament, the Apostle Paul put it this way: "For by grace you have been saved through faith; and that not of yourselves, it is the gift of God; not as a result of works, that no one should boast" (Ephesians 2:8-9).

Does this mean that good works are irrelevant? By no means! It just means that we cannot use them to justify ourselves before God and make a claim on eternal life. In fact, the Bible makes it clear that we are saved to do good works that will glorify Jesus. In the very passage in Ephesians where Paul states we are saved by grace through faith, and not by works, he proceeds to state: "For we [the Redeemed] are His workmanship, created in Christ Jesus for good works, which God prepared beforehand, that we should walk in them" (Ephesians 2:10).

Paul repeated this point in his letter to Titus when he stated that Jesus "gave Himself for us, that He might redeem us from every lawless deed and purify for Himself a people for His own possession, zealous for good deeds" (Titus 2:14). Paul concluded that letter by saying that those who have been justified by grace (the free gift of God), should be "careful to engage in good deeds" (Titus 3:7-8).

James, the brother of Jesus, made the same point in his sermon to the Church when he taught that "faith without works is dead" (James 2:26).

The message of these scriptures is that we are not saved by works, but we are saved to do good works. Accordingly, our eternal destiny will not be determined by our works, but for those who are saved, their good works will be recognized with special rewards (Matthew 16:27 and Romans 2:5-7).

So, if people cannot work their way to Heaven, how then can they be saved? Paul answered this question in Romans 10:9 when he wrote: "If you confess with your mouth Jesus as Lord, and believe in your heart that God raised Him from the dead, you shall be saved." The hope of Heaven depends upon your placing your faith in Jesus as your Lord and Savior (John 3:16).

The Bible says "the wages of sin is death" (Romans 6:23). The same verse says eternal life is a "free gift of God . . . in Christ Jesus our Lord." Every person who has ever lived, except one, has been a sinner and therefore deserving of death. Jesus is the only person who ever lived a sinless life (1

Peter 2:21-22) and therefore did not deserve to die. Thus, when He died, He did so because He took our sins upon Himself, dying for us that we might be reconciled to God the Father through faith in Him (1 Peter 2:24 and 2 Corinthians 5:21).

2) But I am a very good man. I'm faithful to my wife. I am attentive to my children. I'm an honest and diligent employee, I provide well for my family, and I pay my taxes. I even do volunteer work for our local hospital, and I assist the Boy Scouts with fund raising. Surely a just God would not overlook these good works in my life.

You are right when you say God is just (Deuteronomy 32:4). And as a just God, He must deal with the sin in our lives. The Bible says God deals with sin in one of two ways — either grace or wrath (John 3:36). Every person on this planet is under either the grace or wrath of God. The only way to become a candidate of God's grace is to put your faith in His Son as your Lord and Savior.

As to your good works, I would suggest that you compare them to the good deeds of a man named Cornelius. His story is told in Acts chapter 10. He was a Roman soldier stationed in Israel, and although he was a representative of a cruel oppressor, he was so devout and generous that he was highly respected by the Jewish people. He is described as a man "who feared God . . . and prayed to God continually" (Acts 10:1-2). He is further described as "a righteous and God-fearing man well spoken of by the entire nation of the Jews" (Acts 10:22). But despite all this, he was spiritually lost. He needed a Savior.

So, God sent the Apostle Peter to witness Jesus to him and all his household. Peter was welcomed by Cornelius, and Peter proceeded to share with him the good news that Jesus had died for his sins and had been resurrected and had been "appointed by God as Judge of the living and dead" (Acts

10:34-43). Cornelius and all his household responded to this message by accepting Jesus as Lord and Savior (Acts 10:44-48).

Cornelius, despite all his righteousness and good works, still needed a Savior.

3) But I know several Christians who go to church regularly, and I know from observation that I'm a better person than they are. How could they be saved and I be lost?

Because God does not grade on the curve; He grades on the Cross. You can always find someone worse than you, but that will never justify you before God.

Further, you must keep in mind that Christians are not perfect people. They are sinners who have recognized their sinful condition and their need of a Savior. By placing their faith in Jesus, they have been spiritually regenerated and sealed for salvation, but they have not yet been perfected. They still dwell in a carnal body with all its fleshly desires.

But when they accepted Jesus, they received the indwelling of the Holy Spirit (Acts 2:38), and the Spirit is working within them to shape them more fully each day into the image of Jesus (2 Corinthians 3:17-18).

4) What about "once saved, always saved"? Do you believe that?

This is probably one of the most frequently asked questions at my Bible prophecy forums, even though it is not directly related to Bible prophecy.

When the question is asked in a public forum, I always avoid answering it because I have found that it is an explosive topic that is not productive to deal with publicly. So, I usually answer the question by saying, "I'm sorry, but your question is not relevant to Bible prophecy, so I would suggest that you discuss it with your pastor."

For those of you who may not be familiar with the issue, it is a debate between those with an Armenian viewpoint and those with a Calvinist view. The Armenian argues that it is possible for a Christian to "fall from grace" and thus become lost. The Calvinist argues that once a person is saved, it is not possible for him or her to lose their salvation.

I believe the extremes of both viewpoints are unbiblical. The extreme Armenian will argue that every time you sin, you lose your salvation unless you immediately repent. I grew up in a church that taught this theology, so I know it well. It creates an acute sense of spiritual insecurity and contributes to emotional instability. As a kid, I remember witnessing people coming forward time and time again at our church services to confess their sins and be re-baptized over and over, to make sure they were saved.

The ultra-Calvinist position is just as bad in my opinion. According to this theology, God predetermines who is going to be saved and who is going to be lost, and there is nothing anyone can do to change their fate. To me, this concept makes God out to be a monster.

I ran across a tragic example of this view several years ago when I was listening to an audio tape of a sermon that had been delivered at a Baptist Church in Denton, Texas. The guest speaker, who was a well-known theologian, began his sermon by asking, "How many of you here this morning have received Jesus as your Lord and Savior?" After a brief pause (during which I imagine most of the people present raised their hands), the preacher said, "I have bad news for you. Everyone of you who raised your hand is lost because you are too naturally depraved to receive Jesus of your own free will. You are therefore trusting in your own works. The fact of the matter is that God has either predestined you to be saved, or He has not, and there is nothing you can do about it."

When it comes to more moderate views on both sides, I could present a seemingly iron-clad argument in behalf of either position, depending on the verses of Scripture I chose to use. And I have found that when that is the case, the truth of the matter usually lies somewhere in the middle.

Here's where I have come out on the issue. I believe we are saved by faith apart from works, and I believe we are kept in a saved condition by faith apart from works. But I do not believe that when I accepted Jesus in faith that I surrendered my free will and became a robot. I believe I still have the freedom to reject my faith in word or in deed — in word, by renouncing Jesus; in deed, by persisting to live in open sin.

As long as I am walking in faith with the Lord, I can say with absolute confidence that I am saved. But I believe it is possible for me to lose that faith, and I base that conclusion on experience as well as the Scriptures.

In my experience I have seen far too many professing Christians walk away from their faith, abandoning their families and getting in bed with the world. I recently read the testimony of a Muslim imam (spiritual leader) who for many years was a Southern Baptist pastor. For years he taught that Jesus was God in the flesh and that our only hope of salvation was through putting our faith in Jesus as Lord and Savior. Today, he denies the divinity of Jesus and argues that He was just a great prophet preparing the way for the greatest prophet, Mohammed.

Those who believe in "once saved, always saved," respond to examples like this by quoting 1 John 2:19 where the Apostle John states that some apostates who had left the Church had done so because "they were not really one of us." In other words, moderate Calvinists will always argue that those who renounce their Christian faith or who become apostate in their beliefs, never were true Christians in the first place.

I'm sure this is true in many cases, but I'm also equally sure it is not true in all cases. I say that with confidence because there are scriptures which, in my opinion, make it clear that a true believer can fall from grace. Take, for example, 1 Corinthians 15:1-2. In this passage Paul speaks of the gospel he had preached, "by which also you are saved, if you hold fast the word which I preached to you." *If?* The New Testament is full of such conditional statements. Consider Hebrews 3:12-14 —

> 12) Take care, brethren, that there not be in any one of you an evil, unbelieving heart that falls away from the living God.
>
> 13) But encourage one another, day after day, as long as it is still called "Today," so that none of you will be hardened by the deceitfulness of sin.
>
> 14) For we have become partakers of Christ, if we hold fast the beginning of our assurance firm until the end . . .

Christians are being warned in this passage to resist evil lest they become hardened by sin. And they are further warned to hold fast in their faith until the end. Why the warning if there is no danger in falling away from the faith?

This is a persistent theme throughout the book of Hebrews. For example, in chapter 6 there is reference to those who once were "enlightened and have tasted of the heavenly gift and have been partakers of the Holy Spirit" and then have "fallen away" (Hebrews 6:4-6) How can anyone be a partaker of the Holy Spirit without being born again? This has to be speaking of a true Christian.

In like manner, the Apostle Peter describes people who have "escaped the defilements of the world by the knowledge of the Lord and Savior Jesus Christ" and then have become entangled once again in the world. He says their latter state is worse than their first, observing, "it would be better for them not to have known the way of righteousness, than having known it, to turn away." He concludes with a vivid illustration, saying that such persons are like a dog who "returns to its own vomit" (2 Peter 2:20-22).

There is another reason I don't like to spend time dealing with this issue. That's because when you get down to the bottom line, the two moderate viewpoints agree!

I'll explain what I mean with an illustration. Let's consider a fellow — we will call him Tom — who has never had any religious experience in his life. He marries a believing woman, and she starts pressing him to go to church with her. He finally agrees, and the message touches his heart and convicts him. He spends several days reading the Bible and then calls the pastor to inform him that he has decided to accept Jesus as his Lord and Savior.

The next Sunday he goes forward and makes his confession. He is baptized, and he starts attending church faithfully and gets involved in an in-depth Bible study. Within two years he has become a deacon of the church and one of its youth leaders.

And then, one night while surfing the Internet, he accidently lands on a porn site and decides to take a peek. In a short time he is addicted. His wife discovers the situation when they receive a credit card bill with over $500 in charges from porn sites. He confesses and asks her forgiveness, but the problem continues, and soon his children discover pornographic videos he has hidden in a cabinet.

The marriage breaks up. Tom begins drinking. He soon moves in with a woman who proves to be a drug dealer. A year later he is found dead from a drug overdose.

The moderate Calvinist would say, "He was never saved in the first place." The moderate Armenian would contend that "he fell from grace." Both would agree he was lost. So, why all the argument?

5) Do you believe our pets will be with us in Heaven?

This is always one of the first questions to come up when talking about Heaven. I get the question constantly from people who are grieving over the loss of a dear pet. And I know their feeling, for I have lost several pets in my lifetime whom I loved very much.

The eternal fate of animals is a question the Bible does not directly answer. What we can say with certainty is that God loves His creation, including the animals:

Revelation 4:11 tells us that all things were created for God's pleasure.

Matthew 10:29 says that even when a little sparrow falls to the ground, God notices.

Luke 12:6 says that God never forgets about the animals.

Psalm 104:21-30 and Matthew 6:26 describe how God Himself feeds the animals.

Job 12:10 assures us that "In His hand is the life of every creature."

Another thing we can say with certainty is that God is determined to restore all of creation — both the plant and animal kingdoms — to the original perfection they enjoyed before being corrupted by the sin of Man (Acts 3:21 and Romans 8:19-21).

Jesus died not only to redeem Mankind, but to redeem the creation. This was emphasized prophetically in the Hebrew Scriptures in a symbolic way. When the High Priest would enter the Holy of Holies once a year to sprinkle blood on the mercy seat of the Ark of the Covenant, the book of Leviticus tells us that he would take a step back and sprinkle some of the blood on the ground in front of the Ark (Leviticus 16:15).

Why did he do this? The blood on the mercy seat was a prophecy that one day the blood of the Messiah would make it possible for the grace of God to cover the law of God (the tablets of law rested in the Ark under the lid called the mercy seat). The blood on the ground was a prophecy that the sacrifice of the Messiah would also make it possible for God to lift the curse that rests on creation and redeem all of it to its original perfection.

With regard to specific scriptures, Luke 3:6 says: "And all flesh will see the salvation of God." Some translations say "all people," but the key Greek word here is *sarx* which is inclusive of all flesh, including animals.

There is also an interesting statement in Psalm 104. Speaking of animals, the psalm says:

29) You take away their spirit, they expire
   And return to their dust.

30) You send forth Your Spirit, they are created;
   And you renew the face of the ground.

In response to this passage, Randy Alcorn in his book, *Heaven,* asks: "What does God mean that He sends His Spirit and creates them?" He concludes that the passage is talking about "re-creating animals after they've died."[3] As he points out, the same "they" who die are the "they" who are created or re-created as part of the earth's renewal. This is perhaps part of what Jesus meant when He said that His return would be the time of "regeneration" (Matthew 19:28).

We know that animals exist in Heaven now (Revelation 4:6-8). We also know for certain that animals will exist on earth during the millennial reign of Jesus (Isaiah 11:6-9), and we are told that all animals will become herbivorous once again. The wolf will lie down with the lamb. The lion will eat straw with the ox. A little child will play in the cobra's hole because the cobra will no longer be poisonous (Isaiah 11:8). I have a picture of the "peaceable kingdom" hanging behind my desk. It shows a little boy in a white robe walking down a road with a lion on a leash. The lion will be a pet instead of a threat.

The Bible tells us very little about the Eternal State that will follow our Lord's millennial reign. All we know for certain is that the Redeemed will live in new bodies on a new earth in the presence of Almighty God, serving Him and experiencing intimate fellowship with Him. The book of Revelation says we will "see His face" (Revelation 22:4). Animals are not mentioned in the eternal context.

But that does not mean they will be absent. Randy Alcorn argues they will be present according to what he calls "the principle of redemptive continuity."[4]

Romans 8:18 says that the sufferings of this present age cannot be compared to the glory that is yet to be revealed to us. I suspect that one of the many delightful surprises God will give to the Redeemed will be the joyful companionship of the pets they knew and loved here on this earth. I hope so.

6) Will we be married in Heaven?

No, we will not. Jesus said that when we are resurrected and receive our glorified bodies, we will be like angels in the sense that we will neither marry nor procreate (Matthew 22:30).

This does not mean that a husband and wife will no longer know each other in Heaven. Nor does this mean that a husband and wife will not have a close relationship in Heaven. What it does mean is that they will no longer be married in Heaven.

God established marriage to provide Man with intimate fellowship and to provide for procreation. There will be no need for procreation in Heaven, and Man's need for intimate fellowship will be provided by his perfect fellowship with God and his fellow saints.

7) Will we be angels in Heaven?

No, angels are eternal spirit beings created by God (Colossians 1:15-17). They were never human beings, and we will never be angels. The Bible says that one of the purposes of angels today is to "render service" to those who are saved (Hebrews 1:14). The Bible also says that the Redeemed will one day judge the angels (1 Corinthians 6:3).[5]

Sinners, Turn, Why Will Ye Die?

A Hymn by Charles Wesley

Sinners, turn, why will ye die?
God, your Maker, asks you why?
God, who did your being give,
Made you with Himself to live —
He the fatal cause demands,
Asks the work of His own hands,
Why, ye thankless creatures, why
Will ye cross His love, and die?

Sinners, turn, why will ye die?
God, your Saviour, asks you why?
God, who did your souls retrieve,
Died Himself, that ye might live;
Will you let Him die in vain?
Crucify your Lord again?
Why, ye ransomed sinners, why
Will you slight His grace, and die?

Dead, already dead within,
Spiritually dead in sin,
Dead to God while here you breathe,
Pant ye after second death?*
Will you still in sin remain,
Greedy of eternal pain?
O ye dying sinners, why,
Why will you for ever die?

*Note: The "second death" is a phrase used in the book of Revelation to refer to Hell. Those who die outside a faith relationship with God are destined to a second death by being consigned to Hell (Revelation 20:14).

Chapter 4

Is Hell For Real?

"Do not fear those who kill the body, but are unable to kill the soul; but rather fear Him who is able to destroy both soul and body in Hell." — Matthew 10:28

Many people consider Hell to be nothing more than a curse word or a joke.

I'm constantly hearing people on television saying, "I'm going to party in Hell!" They say it with gusto, as if they are bragging about a great accomplishment. Conan O'Brien, the former host of NBC's *Late Night Show*, wrote and performed a song mocking Hell. The song is so perverse that only parts can be quoted. The following section will give you the idea:[1]

I'm gonna go to Hell when I die
I'm gonna go to Hell when I die.

I can't be saved, it's too late for me
I'm going to H-E Double L when I D-I-E
You could say I'm messed up, but I'm keepin' it real
I'll sleep with your mom for a home cooked meal
Give a guy with no legs a new pair of shoes
And give Ben Affleck a bottle of booze
I call up Nick Lechey, tell him he's gay
Then ask Jessica to spell Chevrolet

I'm gonna go to Hell when I die
I'm gonna go to Hell when I die

When the movie star Tom Hanks was asked about his collaborative efforts with director Ron Howard, he said, "Ron Howard is a great man, and a great director. I would follow Ron Howard all the way to Hell."[2] Cable television's Ted Turner mocked Hell in a similar manner when he said, "I don't need anybody to die for me. I've had a few drinks and a few girlfriends, and if that's gonna put me in Hell, then so be it."[3]

The Australian hard rock band, AC/DC, released an album in 1979 titled, *Highway to Hell*. The title song bragged about their determination to end up in Hell:[4]

>Living easy, living free
>Season ticket on a one way ride
>Asking nothing, leave me be
>Taking everything in my stride
>Don't need reason, don't need rhyme
>Ain't nothing I would rather do
>Going down, party time
>My friends are gonna be there too
>I'm on the highway to Hell
>
>I'm on the highway to Hell
>No stop signs or speed limit
>Nobody's gonna slow me down
>Like a wheel, gonna spin it
>Nobody's gonna mess me round
>Hey, Satan paid my dues
>Playing in a rocking band
>Hey, Momma, look at me
>I'm on the way to the promised land
>I'm on the highway to Hell

The general attitude about Hell has been perhaps best expressed by the blasphemous and foul-mouthed comedian, George Carlin (1937-2008):[5]

> Religion has actually convinced people that there's an invisible man — living in the sky — who watches everything you do, every minute of every day. And the invisible man has a special list of ten things he does not want you to do. And if you do any of these ten things, he has a special place, full of fire and smoke and burning and torture and anguish, where he will send you to live and suffer and burn and choke and scream and cry forever 'til the end of time . . . but he loves you!

Carlin's remark about Hell is an interesting one because it pretty well summarizes why I believe most pastors rarely ever preach about Hell. I'm convinced that most find it difficult to talk about a just and loving God who is going to torture lost people eternally.

There is no doubt about it — Hell has been trivialized by the world and ignored by the Church. But Hell was a very important topic to Jesus. He spoke about it repeatedly, whereas he spoke of Heaven very seldom.

The Reality of Hell

The Bible presents Hell, like Heaven, as a real place. The Bible says that God created this terrible place to serve as the ultimate destiny of the Devil and his angels (Matthew 25:41). The Bible also teaches that Hell will be the destiny of all people who reject the grace and mercy God has provided through Jesus and who choose, instead, to follow Satan (Matthew 25:46).

Hell is described in the Scriptures as a place of darkness and sadness (Matthew 22:13), a place of fire (Matthew 5:22), a place of torment (Revelation 14:10), a place of destruction (Matthew 7:13), and a place of disgrace and everlasting contempt (Daniel 12:2).

Its Distinction from Hades

Hell is not Hades. A careful study of the Scriptures will reveal that Hades in the New Testament is the same place as Sheol in the Old Testament (Psalm 49:15).

Before the Cross, Hades (or Sheol) was the holding place for the spirits of the dead who awaited their resurrection, judgment, and ultimate consignment to Heaven or Hell. According to Jesus' story of the rich man and Lazarus (Luke 16:19-31), Hades was composed of two compartments — Paradise and Torments. At death, the spirits of the righteous (those who had put their faith in God) went to a compartment in Hades called Paradise. The unrighteous went to a compartment called Torments. The two compartments were separated by a wide gulf that could not be crossed.

The Bible indicates that the nature of Hades was radically changed at the time of the Cross. After His death on the Cross, Jesus descended into Hades and declared to all the spirits there His triumph over Satan through the shedding of His blood for the sins of Mankind (1 Peter 3:18-19; 4:6).

The Bible also indicates that after His resurrection, when He ascended to Heaven, Jesus took Paradise with Him, transferring the spirits of the righteous dead from Hades to Heaven (Ephesians 4:8-9 and 2 Corinthians 12:1-4). The spirits of the righteous dead are thereafter pictured as being in Heaven before the throne of God (Revelation 6:9 and 7:9).

Thus, since the time of the Cross, the spirits of dead saints no longer go to Hades. They are taken, instead, directly to Heaven. The spirits of Old Testament saints could not go directly to Heaven because their sins had not been forgiven. Their sins had only been covered, so to speak, by their faith. Their sins could not be forgiven until Jesus shed His blood for them on the Cross.

The souls of the unrighteous dead will remain in Hades until the end of the millennial reign of Jesus. At that time they will be resurrected and judged at the Great White Throne Judgment portrayed in Revelation 20:11-15. They will be judged by their works, and since no person can be justified before God by works (Ephesians 2:8-10), all the unrighteous will be cast into Hell, which the passage in Revelation refers to as "the lake of fire" (Revelation 20:14).

The Duration of Hell

How long will the unrighteous be tormented in Hell? The traditional view holds that Hell is a place of eternal, conscious torment. According to this view, a person who ends up in Hell is doomed to a never-ending existence of excruciating pain and suffering. Hell is a place of no escape and no hope.

Another point of view — the one I hold — takes the position that immortality is conditional, depending upon one's acceptance of Christ. I believe the Bible teaches the unrighteous will be resurrected, judged, punished in Hell for a period of time proportional to their sins, and then suffer destruction (the death of body and soul).

In a moment we will take a brief look at both views, but before we do, I would like to remind us all of a sobering truth: Hell is a reality, and it is a dreadful destiny. Hell exists because God cannot be mocked (Galatians 6:7). He is going to deal with sin, and He deals with sin in one of two ways — either grace or wrath. John 3:36 says, "He who believes in the Son has eternal life; but he who does not obey the son shall not see life, but the wrath of God abides on him."

Whatever we conclude from the Scriptures about the duration of Hell, we must remember that Hell is to be avoided at all costs. Whether the wicked suffer there eternally or are destroyed after enduring God's terrible punishment, Hell is an unimaginably terrifying place.

We must also remember that our beliefs about the duration of Hell are not on the plane of cardinal doctrine. Sincere, godly Christians may study the same scripture passages about Hell and end up with differing conclusions about the issue of its duration. Our varied viewpoints, arrived at through earnest and godly study, should not be allowed to cause division or rancor in the body of Christ.

The Traditional Viewpoint

Few traditionalists are happy about the doctrine of the eternal torment of the wicked, but they accept it anyway because they believe it to be biblical. In this they are to be commended.

Most point to scriptures such as Matthew 25:46 for support: "Then these [the wicked] will go away into eternal punishment, but the righteous into eternal life." Since the word "eternal" is used of both the wicked and the righteous, they conclude that the punishment must be eternal in the same way that the life is.

Many traditionalists also cite Revelation 20:10 — a verse specifically about the Devil, the Antichrist and the False Prophet — to prove that a God of love can indeed sentence at least some of His creatures to eternal torment: "And the devil who deceived them was thrown into the lake of fire and brimstone, where the beast and the false prophet are also; and they will be tormented day and night forever and ever." If it is possible for God to treat one set of His creatures in this way, they reason, why should it be impossible for Him to do the same thing with another set?

Still another Revelation passage also figures in the traditionalist argument. Revelation 14:9-11 reads:

> 9) And another angel, a third one, followed them, saying with a loud voice, "If anyone worships the beast and his image, and receives

a mark on his forehead or upon his hand,

10) he also will drink of the wine of the wrath of God, which is mixed in full strength in the cup of His anger; and he will be tormented with fire and brimstone in the presence of the holy angels and in the presence of the Lamb.

11) And the smoke of their torment goes up forever and ever; and they have no rest day and night, those who worship the beast and his image, and whoever receives the mark of his name."

Traditionalists notice that not only are these unbelievers tossed into the lake of fire where "the smoke of their torment goes up forever and ever," but they have no rest "day or night." This is in stark contrast to the saved, who will enjoy rest eternally (Revelation 14: 13). To traditionalists, both the "rest" of believers and the "unrest" of unbelievers seem to imply a conscious, eternal state.

Other Traditionalist Arguments

In other parts of the Bible, several passages which talk about Hell use the word "destroy" or "destruction" to describe what happens to the unrighteous. Traditionalists claim that the picture in these passages is not of obliteration but of a ruin of human life out of God's presence forever. In this way they are able to conceive of a "destruction" which lasts forever.

A more philosophical traditionalist argument concerns Mankind's creation in the image of God. Some traditionalists believe that the torments of Hell must be eternal, since humankind was made in the image of God and that image cannot be "uncreated." Thus they believe that immortality was bestowed on Mankind when God created male and female in His image.

Last, many traditionalists believe that Hell must be eternal because of the nature of sin itself. All sin is an offense against God, goes this argument, and since God is infinite, all sin is infinitely odious. Jonathan Edwards (1703-1758), the great Puritan theologian, took this line of argument in his famous sermon, "The Justice of God in the Damnation of Sinners."[6]

As you can see, these arguments seem both biblical and substantial. And yet they are not without significant problems. Allow me to explain why I believe the conditionalist approach is a better solution to the difficulty.

The Conditionalist Viewpoint

The doctrine of the duration of Hell has been so strongly held throughout the history of Christianity that few have dared to challenge it. Adding to the reluctance has been the fact that most modern challenges have come from the cults. Thus, a person who dares to question the traditional viewpoint runs the risk of being labeled a cultist.

A classic characteristic of modern-day "Christian" cults is their denial of the reality of Hell. Some argue that everyone will be saved. Most take the position that the unrighteous are annihilated at physical death.

The views of the cults regarding Hell have always been repulsive to me because they deny the clear teaching of Scripture that the unrighteous will be sent to a place of suffering called Hell. Yet, I have never been able to fully embrace the traditional viewpoint of conscious, eternal punishment.

Traditionalist Difficulties

My first difficulty with the traditional view is that it seems to impugn the character of God. I kept asking myself, "How could a God of grace, mercy and love torment the vast majority of humanity eternally?" It did not seem to me to be either loving or just. I realize He is a God of righteousness, holiness and justice, but is eternal suffering justice? The concept of eternal torment seems to convert the true God of justice into a cosmic sadist.

Second, the concept of eternal torment seems to run contrary to biblical examples. God destroyed Sodom and Gomorrah with fire — suddenly and quickly. He destroyed Noah's evil world with water — suddenly and quickly. He ordered the Canaanites to be killed swiftly. In the Law of Moses there was no provision for incarceration or torture. Punishments for violation of the Law consisted either of restitution or death. Even sacrificial animals were spared suffering through precise prescriptions for their killing that guaranteed a death that would be as quick and painless as possible.

As a student of God's Prophetic Word, I found a third problem with the traditional view. It seems to contradict a descriptive phrase that is used in prophecy to describe Hell. That term is "the second death." It is a term peculiar to the book of Revelation (Revelation 2:11; 20:6, 14; 21:8). How can Hell be a "second death" if it consists of eternal, conscious torment?

The Problem of Destruction

A fourth reason the traditional view has always troubled me is that it seems to ignore an important biblical teaching about Hell; namely, that Hell is a place of destruction. Jesus Himself spoke of Hell as a place of "destruction" (Matthew 7:13). Further, in Matthew 10:28 Jesus said: "Do not fear those who kill the body, but are unable to kill the soul; but rather fear Him who is able to destroy both soul and body in Hell."

Likewise, in 2 Thessalonians 1:9 Paul says that those who do not obey the gospel "will pay the penalty of eternal destruction." The writer of Hebrews says that the unrighteous will experience a terrifying judgment that will result in their consumption by fire (Hebrews 10:27). Even one of the most comforting verses in the Bible speaks of the destruction of the unrighteous: "For God so loved the world, that He gave His only begotten Son, that whoever believes in Him should not *perish*, but have eternal life" (John 3:16, emphasis added).

The traditionalist argument that the word "destroy" or "destruction" should be interpreted as "irreparable loss" seems a stretch to me. It seems much more likely that "destroy" should be taken to mean exactly that.

The Meaning of Punishment

Fifth, there is a difference between eternal punishment and eternal punishing. It is one thing to experience a punishment that is eternal in its consequences; it is another thing to experience eternal punishing.

The Bible also speaks of eternal judgment (Hebrews 6:2). Is that a judgment that continues eternally, or is it a judgment with eternal consequences? Likewise, the Bible speaks of eternal redemption (Hebrews 9:12). But this does not mean that Christ will continue the act of redemption eternally. That act took place at the Cross, once and for all. It was an eternal redemption because the result of the redemption had eternal consequences.

Symbolism

Sixth, I noted earlier that traditionalists often cite Revelation 14:9-11 to demonstrate that the suffering of the wicked will be eternal. They most often highlight two phrases. The first refers to those who take the mark of the beast during the Tribulation, who will be "tormented with fire and brimstone in the presence of the holy angels." The second is that "the smoke of their torment goes up forever and ever." Notice that this passage does not speak of eternal torment. Rather, it speaks of "the smoke of their torment" ascending forever.

The Bible is its own best interpreter, and when you look up statements similar to this you will find that they are symbolic for a punishment that has eternal consequences, not a punishment that continues eternally. For example, consider Isaiah 34:10 which speaks of the destruction of Edom. It says the smoke of Edom's destruction will "go up forever."

I have been to Edom (the southern portion of modern day Jordan in the area around Petra). I have seen its destruction. But there was no smoke ascending to heaven. The reference to eternal smoke is obviously symbolic, indicating that Edom's destruction will give eternal testimony to how God deals with a sinful society.

The same is true of Jude 7 when it says that Sodom and Gomorrah experienced "the punishment of eternal fire." Again, I have been to the area at the southern tip of the Dead Sea where these twin cities existed. The area is one of utter devastation, but there is no smoke going up to heaven. They are not burning eternally. They simply suffered a fiery destruction that had eternal consequences.

Immortality

Last, many traditionalists believe that the soul is immortal. But is it? I believe the Bible very specifically denies the immortality of the soul.

In 1 Timothy 6:15-16 Paul says that God alone possesses immortality. And 1 Corinthians 15:53 teaches that the Redeemed will not become immortal until the time of their resurrection.

In other words, immortality is a gift of God which He gives in His grace to the Redeemed at the time of their resurrection. There is no need to believe in an eternal Hell if the soul is not intrinsically immortal. And it isn't.

A Summary

You should see by now that both the traditional and conditional positions on Hell can muster good, biblical support for their point of view. We are not talking here about a biblical view versus an unbiblical one.

In defining any doctrine, everything the Bible has to say about the issue must be considered. Concerning the issue of Hell, the only way I have been able to incorporate all that the Bible has to say is to conclude:

1) Those who die outside a faith relationship with Jesus are initially confined to a compartment in Hades called Torments.

2) At the end of the Millennium, they will be resurrected and judged of their works by Jesus at the Great White Throne Judgment.

3) All of them will be condemned to Hell because no one can be justified before God by their works.

4) They will be cast into the lake of fire (Hell) where they will suffer a time of torment in proportion to their sins.

5) They will then experience the "second death" (death of body, soul and spirit).

The Reality of Hell

Which viewpoint is right— the traditional one or the conditionalist concept? I have cast my vote for the conditionalist understanding. You may decide that the evidence points in the other direction. That's okay. The important thing to keep in mind is that Hell is a reality, and regardless of its specific nature, it is a terrible destiny.

And because it is a horrible reality, it needs to be preached. People need to know the consequence of rejecting

God's love, grace, and mercy.

The story has been told of C. S. Lewis listening to a young preacher's sermon on the subject of God's judgment on sin. At the end of his message, the young man said: "If you do not receive Christ as Savior, you will suffer grave eschatalogical ramifications!"

After the service, Lewis asked him, "Did you mean that any person who doesn't believe in Christ will go to Hell?"

"Precisely," the young preacher responded.

"Then say so," Lewis replied.

The stakes are too great to beat around the bush.

Questions and Answers

1) Doesn't the story of the rich man and Lazarus in Luke 16:19-31 teach eternal torment in Hell?

No, it does not. In fact, eternal torment is not even mentioned. Furthermore, the story has nothing to do with Hell. It is a depiction of Hades as it existed before the Cross, when Paradise was still one of its compartments.

The confusion stems from the fact that some translations state in verse 23 that the rich man was in Hell. That is incorrect. The actual word used in the Greek text is Hades and not Gehenna, the word for Hell.

When unsaved people die, their souls go to a compartment in Hades called Torments where they are subjected to suffering. That particular suffering will come to an end at the conclusion of the Millennial reign of Jesus. At that time He will judge those who are in Hades and consign them to Hell (Revelation 20:11-15). We are told that Hades will be cast into the "lake of fire," which is Hell (Revelation 20:14).

For those who have suffered for lengthy times in Hades, their suffering may well end instantly when they are consigned to Hell where they will experience "eternal destruction" (2 Thessalonians 1:9). Others will likely continue to suffer for a period of time in Hell before they "perish" (John 3:16).

The Bible clearly teaches that there will be degrees of punishment, so some will suffer longer and more intensely than others (Luke 12:35-48, Luke 20:45-47, and Hebrews 10:29).

2) Didn't Jesus teach eternal torment when He said that Hell is a place "where their worm does not die, and the fire is not quenched?" (Mark 9:48)

Jesus could not have been teaching eternal torment when He made this statement because He was quoting Isaiah 66:24 which says that the redeemed will be able to view the corpses of those who are lost. The phraseology about the worm and the fire is figurative language that emphasizes the fact that the testimony of what happens to unrepentant sinners will never die.

Similar wording is used about the destruction of Sodom and Gomorrah. Jude 7 tells us that these cities experienced "the punishment of eternal fire." That does not mean an eternally burning fire; rather, it speaks of a fire with eternal consequences.

3) What about those during the Tribulation who take the mark of the beast? Doesn't the Bible say they will be tormented forever? (Revelation 14:9-11)

Again, there is no mention of eternal torment in these verses. We are told that they will "be tormented in the presence of the holy angels and in the presence of the Lamb" (Revelation 14:10), but no duration of this torment is given. To conclude that the torment will continue eternally, one would have to assume that the soul is immortal. But the Bible denies the immortality of the soul (1 Timothy 6:13-16).

The passage does say that "the smoke of their torment will go up forever," but that is a figurative expression that denotes an eternal witness of their fate. For example, we are told in Isaiah 34:10 that the smoke from Edom's destruction will rise forever. There is no such smoke rising from Edom today except in the sense that we have the memory of its destruction.

4) What about the Antichrist and the False Prophet? Doesn't the Bible say they will be subjected to eternal torment? (Revelation 19:20 and 20:10).

Yes, Revelation 20:10 states that the Antichrist and his False Prophet will "be tormented forever and ever," together with Satan. But this certainly is no indication that the rest of humanity will suffer eternal torment.

The Antichrist and False Prophet are two special cases. Keep in mind that they will be responsible for the deaths of one-half of humanity during the first three-and-a-half years of the Tribulation. That's a total of 3 billion people in today's terms. They are also going to kill two-thirds of the Jews during the second half of the Tribulation. By the end of the seven years of the Tribulation, it is likely that they will have the blood of two-thirds of humanity on their hands — or 4 billion people. All the carnage of all the nefarious leaders of history — like Hitler, Stalin, and Mao — pales in comparison.

But it may well be that Revelation 20:10 is not speaking of the human beings who will serve as the Antichrist and False Prophet. It may instead be speaking of the demonic spirits that possess them. Note that the passage refers to "the beast and the false prophet." We are told in Revelation 11:7 that the beast "comes up out of the abyss." According to the Scriptures, this is the pit where evil spirits are imprisoned, not human beings. Likewise, the False Prophet is referred to as "another beast" (Revelation 13:11), meaning another of the same kind.

5) Won't the Conditional viewpoint motivate people to ignore God?

Let me quote Edward Fudge's answer to this question: "Only if their only reason for serving God is the belief that He will inflict on the wicked a torture unimaginably worse than the most monstrous tyrant among men ever dreamed of inflicting on his victims.

"The truth is that the traditional doctrine of everlasting torture in Hell has created more atheists than almost anything else Christians have ever taught . . .

"What the Conditionalist view does is magnify the justice of God (each doomed sinner receives precisely what he or she deserves and nothing else), the mercy of God (even the worst sinner finally perishes forever), and the holiness of God (His wrath is real, but it is measured with exact precision in keeping with His own character)."[7]

6) Doesn't the Conditionalist viewpoint require a lot of spiritualization of the Scriptures?

Not at all. In fact, it is the traditional view of everlasting torment that requires the most spiritualization. Those who hold to the traditional concept must spiritualize such words and phrases as "perish," "destruction," "consumed by fire," and "second death."

The Conditionalist view requires only the spiritualization of figurative expressions like "their worm will not die" and "the smoke of their torment will go up forever."

7) Don't the cults hold the Conditionalist viewpoint?

Many, like the Jehovah's Witnesses, believe that the souls of sinners are annihilated at death, but that is not the Conditionalist position. A marginal group, The Seventh Day Adventists, does embrace Conditionalism, but their endorsement of it no more invalidates it than does their endorsement of the Trinity invalidate that thoroughly biblical concept.

8) **What do you consider to be the single most powerful argument against the traditional concept of eternal torment in Hell?**

The fact that the Bible says that Jesus paid the price for our sins (Isaiah 53:5, Galatians 1:4, Hebrews 1:3 and 1 Peter 2:24).

What was that price? It was extreme suffering followed by death. It was not eternal torment. Unrepentant sinners will therefore experience what Jesus experienced: suffering and death (the "Second Death").

The bottom line is that because of a preconceived, unbiblical notion that the soul is immortal, we have read *eternal* torment into the Scriptures when it was never intended for Mankind. Hell was created for Satan and his angels, not for Mankind, and it is Satan and his demonic hordes who will be consigned to Hell and its torments eternally.

Old Buddha

A Song by Mark Farrow

Well, old Buddha was a man
And I'm sure that he did well,
But I pray for his disciples
Lest they end up in hell,
And I'm sure that old Mohammed
Was sure he knew the way,
But it won't be Hari Krishna
We stand before on judgment day.

Chorus:

No, it won't be old Buddha
That's sitting on the throne,
And it won't be old Mohammed
That's calling me home,
And it won't be Hari Krishna
That plays that trumpet tune,
And we're going to see the Son,
Not Reverend Moon!

Well, I don't hate anybody,
So please don't take me wrong,
But there really is a message
In this simple song,
See, there's only one way — Jesus,
If eternal life's your goal,
And meditation of the mind,
It won't save your soul.

Chapter 5

Are There Many Roads To God?

"Let it be known to all of you . . . that by the name of Jesus Christ the Nazarene, whom you crucified, who God raised from the dead . . . there is salvation in no one else; for there is no other name under heaven that has been given among men by which we must be saved." — Acts 4:10-12 (NASV)

"What will happen to those who have never heard the Gospel?" This is one of the most frequent questions I receive. People believe that God is just, and they cannot reconcile that belief with the idea that He might consign a person to Hell who never was given an opportunity to hear the Gospel.

Therefore, increasingly, many Christians are concluding that there must be many roads to God and that sincere Jews and Muslims and Buddhists and others will make it to Heaven.

Crucial Questions

What does the Bible have to say about this important issue? Are those who live and die without hearing the Gospel condemned to an eternity in Hell? And what about those who have put their faith in the god of some religion other than Christianity and who strive to live righteous lives? Are they also condemned to Hell? Is it possible that God has revealed Himself in different ways to different peoples, and therefore there are many different roads to God? Could the sign be true that I saw in a Sunday School class at a church that read: "Our God is too big to be confined to one religion"?

What Jesus Had to Say

Let's begin our search for an answer to these questions by taking a look at what Jesus had to say —

Speaking to the Apostle Thomas, Jesus said, "I am the way, and the truth, and the life; no one comes to the Father, but through Me." — John 14:6

After appointing His twelve Apostles, Jesus said to them: "Everyone therefore who shall confess Me before men, I will also confess him before My Father who is in heaven. But whoever shall deny Me before men, I will also deny him before My Father who is in heaven." — Matthew 10:32-33

Speaking to 70 disciples being sent forth to proclaim the kingdom of God, Jesus said: "The one who listens to you listens to Me, and the one who rejects you rejects Me; and he who rejects Me rejects the One who sent Me." — Luke 10:16

Early in His ministry, while in Jerusalem, Jesus delivered a sermon on His relationship with God the Father, and in it He said: "Truly, truly, I say to you, he who hears My word, and believes Him who sent Me, has eternal life, and does not come into judgment, but has passed out of death into life." — John 5:24

At His last supper with the Apostles, Jesus prayed: "And this is eternal life, that they may know You, the only true God, and Jesus Christ whom You have sent." — John 17:3

And then, of course, there is Jesus' most famous statement about the issue of salvation — the words He spoke to Nicodemus, a Jewish spiritual leader who was a member of the Sanhedrin Council: "For God so loved the world that He gave His only begotten Son, that whoever believes in Him should not perish, but have eternal life." — John 3:16

What conclusion can we draw from these statements? I would propose the following:

1) Jesus is the one and only way to God.

2) Those who put their faith in Jesus as Lord and Savior will be saved.

3) Those who reject Jesus will be condemned, for those who reject Jesus are guilty of rejecting God.

4) The essence of salvation is a personal relationship with Jesus.

What the Apostles Had to Say

These conclusions are affirmed in the writings of the Apostles, as you can see from the following statements —

In the first Gospel sermon ever preached, Peter made a bold assertion: "Therefore, let all the house of Israel know for certain that God has made Him [Jesus] both Lord and Christ [Messiah] — this Jesus whom you crucified." Peter then commanded his audience to "repent and let each of you be baptized in the name of Jesus Christ for the forgiveness of your sins" (Acts 2:36 & 38).

Not long after this, Peter was arrested and hauled before the Sanhedrin Council — the very group of Jewish leaders who had condemned Jesus to death. In his statement to them, he said: "Let it be known to all of you, and to all the people of Israel that by the name of Jesus Christ the Nazarene, whom you crucified, whom God raised from the dead . . . there is salvation in no one else, for there is no other name under heaven that has been given among men by which we must be saved" (Acts 4:10 & 12).

The Apostle Paul affirmed Peter's point in a letter he wrote to Timothy: "God our Savior desires all men to be saved and to come to the knowledge of the truth. For there is one God, and one mediator also between God and men, the man Christ Jesus who gave Himself as a ransom for all . . ." (1 Timothy 2:3-6).

In like manner, the Apostle John confirmed that Jesus is the only hope of salvation when he wrote: "Who is the liar but the one who denies that Jesus is the Christ [Messiah]? This is the antichrist, the one who denies the Father and the Son. Whoever denies the Son does not have the Father; the one who confesses the Son has the Father also" (1 John 2:22-23). John repeated this principle when he added: ". . . God has given us eternal life, and this life is in His Son. He who has the Son has the life; he who does not have the Son of God does not have the life" (1 John 5:11-12).

Again, the conclusions that can be drawn from these statements are self-evident:

1) Jesus was the Messiah — the Savior — promised by God.

2) There is salvation in no other person except Jesus.

3) Those who reject Jesus are guilty of rejecting the Father.

Confirmation of these conclusions can be found in a sermon delivered by John the Baptist in which he proclaimed: "He who believes in the Son has eternal life; but he who does not obey the Son shall not see life, but the wrath of God abides on him" (John 3:36).

John's statement makes it clear that God must deal with sin for He is a just God (Psalm 37:28 and Isaiah 61:8). He deals with sin in one of two ways, either grace or wrath.

Whether or not a person is under grace or wrath depends upon whether he or she has put their faith in Jesus as their Lord and Savior. Those who have done so, have the promise of eternal life. Those who refuse to do so will experience God's wrath.

God's Desire Pertaining to Salvation

But didn't Paul say in 1 Timothy 2:3 that God "desires all men to be saved"? Yes, he did say that, and Peter repeated it in 2 Peter 3:9 where he asserted that "God does not wish that any should perish, but that all should come to repentance."

There is no doubt that it is God's perfect will that all should be saved. But in His permissive will, God allows people to reject His Son and thus be lost. In other words, God does not force anyone to be saved. And because of the depraved nature of Mankind, the vast majority of those who have ever lived will be lost and consigned to Hell as their eternal destiny.

Jesus Himself emphasized this truth in His sermon delivered on the Hill of the Beatitudes in Galilee. Jesus stated His point in no uncertain times: ". . . The gate is wide, and the way is broad that leads to destruction, and many are those who enter by it. For the gate is small, and the way is narrow that leads to life, and few are those who find it . . . Not everyone who says to Me, 'Lord, Lord,' will enter the kingdom of heaven; but he who does the will of My Father who is in heaven" (Matthew 7:13-14 & 21).

The Nature of Man

Again, the Bible emphasizes that the fundamental nature of Man is evil because we are born with a sin nature that puts us in rebellion against the holiness of God. As the prophet Jeremiah put it: "There is nothing more deceitful than the human heart" (Jeremiah 17:9). Likewise, King David wrote: "There is no one who does good . . . they have all turned aside . . . there is no one who does good, not even one" (Psalm 14:1-3). The Apostle Paul affirmed this truth in his letter to the Romans when he quoted David's statement in detail (Romans 3:10-18).

The biblical message is adamant that because of our natural depravity, we have no hope apart from faith in a Savior, and Jesus is that Savior. Isaiah summed it up this way in a prophecy about the promised Messiah: "All of us like sheep have gone astray. Each of us has turned to his own way; but the Lord has caused the iniquity of us all to fall on Him [the Messiah]" (Isaiah 53:6).

The message of the Scriptures is clear. There is only one road to God and that is through Jesus of Nazareth. There is no hope in the modern day false religions of Rabbinical Judaism, Islam, Buddhism, Hinduism, or any of the multitude of natural religions like Animism.

An Important Question

This brings us to a crucial question: Are there any exceptions to the rule that you must place your faith in Jesus in order to be saved?

The answer is yes. Most Christian theologians would agree that there are three groups of people who have been saved without placing their faith in Jesus.

The first group is composed of those children who have died before the age of accountability. The Bible does not specifically state this truth. It is arrived at through deduction from biblical statements.

First, there is the example of King David's child that was born of Bathsheba. When the child died seven days after it was born, David proclaimed by inspiration of the Holy Spirit that although the child could not come back to him, one day he would go to be with the child (2 Samuel 12:23).

The idea that those who die before the age of accountability will be saved is reinforced in the New Testament in the words of Jesus in Matthew 19:13-14 —

> Then some children were brought to Him so that He might lay His hands on them and pray; and the disciples rebuked them. But Jesus said, "Let the children alone, and do not hinder them from coming to Me; for the kingdom of heaven belongs to such as these."

This principle of not holding children accountable for their sins before they know the difference between right and wrong is also reflected in a story in the book of Deuteronomy. When the Israelites balked at entering the Promised Land because they were afraid they would be defeated by the Canaanites, God punished them for not trusting Him by making them wander in the wilderness until the rebellious generation had died off (see Numbers 13 & 14).

The Lord proclaimed that only two people of the current generation would be allowed to enter the land — namely, Caleb and Joshua, the two spies out of twelve who brought back a positive report stating they believed the Lord would defeat their enemies (Deuteronomy 1:34-38). But then, another exception was made: "Moreover, your little ones . . . who this day have no knowledge of good or evil, shall enter there [the Promised Land], and I will give it to them, and they shall possess it" (Deuteronomy 1:39).

Another argument in behalf of the salvation of children who die before the age of accountability is the justice of God. The Bible asserts over and over that our Creator is a God of justice (Zephaniah 3:5). He has an overwhelming passion for justice (Micah 6:8). And He promises repeatedly that justice will be one of the characteristics of His Son's millennial reign (Isaiah 42:1-4). How could a God of perfect justice condemn to Hell children who never knew the difference in right and wrong?

Those who die before the age of accountability will not be eligible to receive special rewards for faithfully serving the Lord, but it appears that they will be granted eternal life. However, this can happen only by having the blood of Jesus applied to them (Hebrews 9:22).

This same exception would apply to the second group — the mentally handicapped who reach adulthood. Since they are incapable of determining right from wrong and are also incapable of repenting and putting their faith in Jesus, it is only reasonable to conclude that a just God would not hold them accountable and would apply the blood of Jesus to their sins.

I have a step-grandson named Jason who falls into this category. At about the age of three a genetic defect was activated that caused his immune system to attack his brain. The effect was a frontal lobotomy that rendered him vegetative. I have since dedicated two books to him. He is a constant reminder to me of the fact that we live in a fallen world. I have no doubt that one day, either at death or at the Rapture, his mind will be set right, and I will be able to enjoy his fellowship eternally.

Another Exception

The third group that has been saved apart from faith in Jesus are those people who lived and died before the birth and revelation of Jesus as God's Son, but who placed their faith in their Creator. Hebrews 11 tells us that people like Abel, Enoch, Noah, and Abraham were justified by their faith in God. They had no Scriptures nor any knowledge of Jesus, yet because they related to their Creator in faith, they were saved. Specifically, Genesis 15:6 says that because Abraham believed the Lord, "it was reckoned to him as righteousness."

Still, each of these people, and many others like them, were dependent upon the sacrifice of Jesus for their salvation to be sealed. Their faith covered their sins, but the forgiveness of their sins depended upon the sacrifice of a perfect person who did not deserve to die. Only the blood of such a person could produce forgiveness of their sins.

That's why Old Testament saints did not go directly to Heaven when they died. They went, instead, to a place called Sheol (Hades in the New Testament), and their souls resided in a compartment called "Abraham's bosom" or "Paradise." They could not be ushered into the presence of a Holy God until their sins were forgiven.

After Jesus' death on the Cross, He descended into Hades and made a proclamation (1 Peter 3:19). We are not told specifically what He said, but most likely it was, "The blood has been shed!" I'm sure those words must have produced a chorus of "Hallelujahs!" We are also told that when Jesus ascended into Heaven, He took a "host of captives" with Him (Ephesians 4:8). In other words, He emptied Hades of those who were saved. Paradise was moved from Hades to Heaven, a reality that Paul later affirmed when he said that he was taken up to "the third heaven," which he identified as Paradise (2 Corinthians 12:1-4).

Another Exception?

This brings us back to one of the questions we began with: What about those today who live and die without ever hearing the Gospel? Are they destined to Hell?

I personally believe the same principle applies to them that applied to people living in Old Testament times before the First Advent of Jesus. Their fate will depend upon whether or not they ever responded to God in faith.

The Bible says that all people have an instinctive knowledge that God exists (Romans 2:14-15). Further, the Bible says that we can realize the existence of God by observing the complexity and beauty of the creation (Psalm 19:1-6).

Because God is a just God (Psalm 89:14), I believe He will hold us responsible for what we knew. Those exposed to the Gospel and reject it will be lost. Those who have only the testimony of instinct and the creation who reject that testimony will also be lost. But those who hear the Gospel and put their faith in Jesus will be saved. And those who respond to the testimony of instinct and the creation by putting their faith in their Creator will also be saved. However, this latter group will be saved only by having the blood of Jesus applied to them as was the case with Old Testament saints.

A Controversial Statement

I believe this is what Billy Graham had in mind in May of 1997 when he made a very controversial statement during an interview of him that was being conducted by Robert Schuller.[1] He said that he believed that God is "calling people out of the world for His name" — including the Muslim world, the Buddhist world, the Christian world and the non-believing world. He added, "They may not even know the name of Jesus, but they know in their hearts that they need something that they don't have, and they turn to the only light they have, and I think that they are saved, and that they're going to be with us in Heaven."

Schuller responded by asking, "What I hear you saying is that it is possible for Jesus Christ to come into human hearts and soul and life, even if they've been born in darkness and have never had exposure to the Bible. Is that a correct interpretation of what you're saying?"

Graham's reply was, "Yes, it is . . . I've met people in various parts of the world in tribal situations, that they have never seen a Bible or heard about a Bible, and never heard of Jesus, but they've believed in their hearts that there was a God, and they've tried to live a life that was quite apart from the surrounding community in which they lived."

These comments by Graham produced a flood of condemnation of him. People accused him of believing in many different roads to God. It is certainly easy to see how his comments could have been misconstrued, but I believe that is exactly what happened.

Billy Graham has never taught that there are many roads to God. On his website (www.billy graham.org) there are two very specific articles about salvation in which Graham affirms his often stated belief that Jesus is the only way to God.[2]

In his controversial statement, which was much too briefly phrased, I think he was only saying that people are going to be judged on the basis of what they knew about God and how they responded to that knowledge, just as was the case in Old Testament times.[3]

Some might respond by saying, "If those who live and die without ever hearing of Jesus might still be saved by their faith in God, whereas those who hear the Gospel and reject it will be lost, then perhaps we should stop proclaiming the Gospel!"

But this statement is based on the faulty assumption that the Gospel is just a fire insurance policy. The truth is that it is much more than that, for the person who receives Jesus as Lord and Savior is blessed with the indwelling power of the Holy Spirit, receiving supernatural power to live triumphantly in a world of heartache and suffering. The person is also enabled to know God personally in this life — an absolutely invaluable blessing.

Further, I believe that any person who would respond to God in faith based on instinct and the witness of the creation is one who would accept the Gospel if exposed to it.

All Professing Christians?

This brings us to another group of people — those professing Christians who have never been born again. What I have in mind are what I prefer to call "Cultural Christians." These are people who claim to be Christians because they profess to believe in Jesus, but they have no personal relationship with Him. Many of these are people who attend church regularly. Some are elders, deacons, teachers, and even pastors. Can they get to Heaven through church membership or by participating in Christian rites like baptism or communion?

The answer of the Bible is a clear "No!" Jesus Himself said that no man can see the kingdom of God unless he be "born again" (John 3:3). That means a person must put his faith in Jesus as his personal Lord and Savior. It is not sufficient to simply believe that Jesus lived. The Bible says that even "the demons believe and shudder" (James 2:19). But they have rejected Jesus as their Lord.

Going to church or participating in Christian rituals is not another road to Heaven. Our churches are filled with unsaved people who are trusting in their works to get them to Heaven. But the Bible says, "For by grace you have been saved through faith . . . not as a result of works, that no one should boast" (Ephesians 2:8-9).

Earlier in this book I mentioned an observation by Dr. Robert Jeffress, pastor of First Baptist Church in Dallas, in which he pointed out that two words sum up one of the fundamental differences between Christianity and all other religions in the world. Those words are "do" and "done." Regarding access to Heaven, all the false religions of the world say, "DO!" Christianity, in stark contrast, proclaims "DONE!"[4] In other words, Christianity declares that Jesus did everything necessary for our salvation through His death on the cross. There is nothing we can add to that.

False expressions of Christianity require you to earn your salvation by doing works that they require. True Christianity says there is nothing you can do to earn your salvation because it is a free gift of God through faith in Jesus as your Lord and Savior. In this sense, true Christianity is really not a religion; rather, it is a relationship. Jesus made this clear at the last supper with His disciples when He prayed to God, saying, ". . . this is eternal life, that they may know You, the only true God, and Jesus Christ whom You have sent" (John 17:3).

In this regard I feel compelled to state, respectfully, that this is an area where Billy Graham seems to have strayed from the Gospel. I say this because he has made it very clear in his writings and his public statements that he believes the Catholic Church is a true expression of Christianity.[5]

This is unfortunate because his endorsement of Catholicism has made many Catholics feel comfortable and safe in their faith. And although I am sure there are some Catholics who have truly placed their faith in Jesus, the vast majority have not because the Catholic Church has always taught salvation by works — which makes the religion of Catholicism a false form of Christianity.[6]

The Bottom Line

From a biblical, Christian perspective, there is no way to escape the conclusion that Jesus is the only way to God, either through direct faith in Him, or by having the blood of Jesus applied to a person who has responded to God in faith through the testimony of instinct and nature.

To argue that there are other roads to God, as some apostate Christian leaders are doing today, is to deny that the sacrifice of Jesus was necessary for the forgiveness of sins. If there really are other roads to God, then Jesus came to earth to die a horrible death for no purpose. His sacrifice was all in vain. Either we are saved by the blood of Jesus, or we are not.

A Glorious Promise Concerning the Future

One thing we know for sure is that every person on earth who is alive at the end of the Tribulation will hear the Gospel before the Second Coming of Jesus. We know this because Jesus said it would happen (Matthew 24:14). That prophecy is being partially fulfilled today through the use of modern technology. Computers are being utilized to rapidly produce translations of the Bible. Satellites are being used to transmit Gospel sermons worldwide.

But the ultimate fulfillment of the prophecy will occur near the end of the Great Tribulation when God will send forth an angel who will circumnavigate the globe and proclaim the Gospel to every person left alive at that time (Revelation 14:6-7). What glorious grace!

Questions and Answers

1) How can you be so intolerant as to say there is only one way to God?

Because it is true. Let me ask you, which is more important, tolerance or truth? Jesus Himself said He was the only way to God (John 14:6), and He was God in the flesh (John 14:9-10). Your argument is with Him and not with me.

Now let me ask you another question: Why do you apply this thinking to religion but not to other aspects of life? Would you apply it to medicine? If a doctor were to tell you there is only one treatment for a disease, would you call him "intolerant"? Is a math teacher intolerant if he insists there is only one proper answer to a math problem?

God has clearly revealed Himself in His creation (Psalm 8:1-3 and Psalm 19:1-2) and in His Word (2 Timothy 3:16-17). He further revealed Himself through His Son by taking on human flesh and going to the Cross to die for our sins (John 1:1-5, 14). What more must He do?

Furthermore, He is no respecter of persons (Romans 2: 11). His gift of salvation through faith in Jesus is available to all people, regardless of race or national origin. What is intolerant about that?

The Bible says that God does not wish that any should perish, and it further says that the only reason Jesus has not yet returned is because God wants to save more people (2 Peter 3:9). It is God's perfect will that all be saved through faith in Jesus, but in His permissive will He allows people to reject His free gift of salvation by placing their faith in false gods.

2) But don't all religions worship the same God?

Absolutely not! There is only one true God (Isaiah 46:9), the God of the Bible, and He is not the god of religions like Islam and Hinduism.

For example, the God of the Bible is repeatedly revealed as a God of love (1 John 4:16). Never once does the Quran call its god, Allah, a god of love. The false god of Islam is aloof and arbitrary, saving whom he pleases and condemning whom he pleases for whatever reason he pleases. He is anything but the loving and personal Father revealed in the Bible (1 Peter 5:6-7).

The same can be said of the god or gods that are worshiped by other religions in the world. Hinduism is another good example. Hindus are both pantheistic and polytheistic. They are pantheistic because Hinduism teaches that all is god and god is all. They are polytheistic because Hinduism maintains that there are many lesser gods.

The god of Rabbinic Judaism is another aloof god who relates to the Jewish nation but not to individual Jews, except the sages who claim to continue to reveal their god's will. Modern day Jews have rejected Jesus as God's Messiah, and they have also rejected the true God of the universe — the triune God consisting of one God in three persons: the Father, the Son, and the Holy Spirit (Matthew 28:19).

In Buddhism, there is no supreme creator god. There are lesser gods, and even Buddha himself is worshiped.

Mormons claim that god is an exalted man and that we can become his equal if we work hard enough. The Jehovah's Witnesses claim that Jesus is in reality the Archangel Michael, a created being, and not everlasting God.

Can all these religions be correct? Of course not! To argue that one is as true as the other is nonsensical. It is nothing but an exercise in political correctness.

3) Why are Christians so intent on converting others to their religion? Why can't they just leave people alone who have another religion?

First of all, Christian evangelists and missionaries are not trying to convert people to another religion, because true Christianity is not a religion, it is a relationship with a person — namely, Jesus Christ. Jesus Himself taught this when He said: "And this is eternal life, that they may know You, the only true God, and Jesus Christ whom You have sent" (John 17:3).

Regarding Christian evangelism — that is, the aggressive efforts of Christians to share their faith — put yourself in the Christian's place for a moment. If you believed that Jesus was God in the flesh and that He is the only way to salvation, wouldn't you want to share that news with others?

In like manner, if you knew the cure to cancer and your next door neighbor developed cancer, wouldn't you have an overwhelming desire to share the cure with him? Surely you wouldn't sit by and calmly watch him die without saying something for fear you might hurt his feelings.

Yet I have seen this happen time and time again, especially with regard to sharing the Gospel with Jews. Well meaning Christians, who understand the persecution Jews have experienced over the years at the hands of misguided Christians, have often taken the position that it is insensitive and even boorish to try to share Jesus with a Jew. The effect is to love Jews right into Hell!

When Christians share the Gospel with non-Christians, they do so out of a sense of love, because they are concerned with the eternal destiny of their souls. If you are a non-Christian and a Christian tries to share Jesus with you, you should feel honored and blessed, and not preyed upon.

True Christians do not share out of a sense of superiority. Their attitude is not one of "I've got something special and therefore I'm better than you." They are motivated purely by a sincere concern for your eternal destiny.

Up From the Grave

A Hymn by Robert Lowry

Low in the grave He lay,
Jesus my Savior.
Waiting the coming day,
Jesus my Lord.

Chorus:

Up from the grave He arose;
With a mighty triumph o'er His foes.
He arose a victor from the dark domain,
And He lives forever
With His saints to reign.
He arose! He arose!
Hallelujah! Christ arose!

Vainly they watch His bed,
Jesus my Savior.
Vainly they seal the dead,
Jesus my Lord.

Death cannot keep its prey,
Jesus my Savior.
He tore the bars away,
Jesus my Lord.

Up from the grave He arose;
With a mighty triumph o'er His foes.
He arose a victor from the dark domain,
And He lives forever
With His saints to reign.
He arose! He arose!
Hallelujah! Christ arose!

Chapter 6

How Can We Be Certain of Life After Death?

"Jesus said to her [Martha] *I am the resurrection and the life; he who believes in Me shall live even if he dies . . ."*— John 11:25 (NASV)

There can be no certainty whatsoever about life after death unless Jesus was raised from the dead. Christianity stands or falls on the truth of Jesus' resurrection, as does any hope of life after death.

The Testimony of Paul

The Apostle Paul made this point clear in his writings. When defining the essence of the Gospel, he wrote that it was the death, burial, and resurrection of Jesus (1 Corinthians 15:3-4).

To make his point crystal clear, he added, ". . . if Christ has not been raised, then our preaching is vain, your faith also is vain" (1 Corinthians 15:14). And then, as if to make certain to get his point across with no misunderstanding, he repeated his assertion, ". . . and if Christ has not been raised, your faith is worthless; you are still in your sins" (1 Corinthians 15:17).

The Testimony of Jesus

Jesus Himself asserted that our hope of resurrection depended upon His own triumph over death. Sixty-five years after His resurrection, He appeared to the Apostle John on the island of Patmos and made this remarkable statement (Revelation 1:17-18):

> Do not be afraid; I am the first and the last,
> and the living One; and I have the keys of
> death and Hades.

Think on that statement for a moment. Jesus is saying, "I am the beginning of history. I am the end of history. I am the meaning of history. And because I have overcome death, I have authority over death (the body) and Hades (the spirit)."

The Testimony of the Apostles

All the apostles recognized fully the significance of Jesus' resurrection, and because of that, His resurrection became the focal point of their preaching.

Peter, in the first Gospel sermon ever preached, reminded his audience that King David had prophesied that the Messiah would be resurrected from the dead (Psalm 16:10). He then proclaimed that Jesus had fulfilled that prophecy: "This Jesus God raised up again, to which we are witnesses" (Acts 2:32).

In Peter's second sermon, delivered on the Temple Mount, He charged his audience with participating in the execution of Jesus by demanding that the "Prince of Life" be put to death, "the one whom God raised from the dead, a fact to which we are witnesses" (Acts 3:14-15).

Peter's third sermon was delivered to the Sanhedrin Council, the very group of Jewish leaders who had condemned Jesus to death. Filled with the Holy Spirit, Peter bravely proclaimed, ". . . let it be known to all of you, and to all the people of Israel, that by the name of Jesus Christ the Nazarene, whom you crucified, whom God raised from the dead . . . there is salvation in no one else" (Acts 4:10, 12).

Speaking of the boldness of the apostles in their preaching, Luke wrote, "And with great power the apostles were giving witness to the resurrection of the Lord Jesus . . ." (Acts 4:33).

When all the apostles were arrested and hauled before the Sanhedrin Council and were threatened if they did not stop preaching, "Peter and the apostles answered and said, 'We must obey God rather than men. The God of our fathers raised up Jesus, whom you had put to death by hanging Him on a cross'" (Acts 5:29-30).

As Stephen, the first Christian martyr, was being stoned to death for his testimony of Jesus, "he gazed intently into Heaven and saw the glory of God, and Jesus standing at the right hand of God, and he said, 'Behold, I see the heavens opened up and the Son of Man standing at the right hand of God'" (Acts 7:55-56).

When Peter was called to preach to Cornelius, the first Gentile convert, he spoke of the crucifixion of Jesus, and then he said, "God raised Him on the third day, and granted that He should become visible, not to all people, but to witnesses who were chosen beforehand by God, that is, to us, who ate and drank with Him after He arose from the dead" (Acts 10:40-41).

When Paul was called and sent forth as a missionary (Acts 13:1-4), his sermons focused on the resurrection as the cardinal event of history, emphasizing that Jesus' resurrection was a fulfillment of prophecy: "And we preach to you the good news of the promise made to the fathers, that God has fulfilled this promise to our children in that He raised up Jesus . . . from the dead, no more to return to decay . . ." (Acts 13:32-34).

In Thessalonica Paul reasoned with the Jews in the synagogue, "explaining and giving evidence that the Christ had to suffer and rise again from the dead . . ." (Acts

17:3).

At Athens, we are told that Paul "was preaching Jesus and the resurrection" (Acts 17:18).

And when Paul was arrested and brought before King Agrippa, he said, "I stand to this day testifying both to small and great, stating nothing but what the Prophets and Moses said was going to take place; that the Christ was to suffer, and that by reason of His resurrection from the dead, He should be the first to proclaim light to both the Jewish people and to the Gentiles (Acts 26:22-23).

As you can see, over and over again the apostles affirmed the resurrection of Jesus and asserted that it is the heart of the Gospel.

Paul's Letters

Accordingly, Paul began his profound theological epistle to the Romans by asserting that he was an apostle called to preach the Gospel concerning Jesus Christ, "who was declared the Son of God with power by the resurrection from the dead . . ." (Romans 1:1-4). Later, in the same letter, Paul stated, ". . . that if you confess with your mouth Jesus as Lord, and believe in your heart that God raised Him from the dead, you shall be saved" (Romans 10:9). And when Paul wrote to his protégé, Timothy, he exhorted him in his teachings to "remember Jesus Christ, raised from the dead, descendant of David, according to my gospel" (2 Timothy 2:8).

In 1 Corinthians 15:5-8 Paul emphasized the validity of the Resurrection by recounting some of the appearances that Jesus made after His resurrection. He states that Jesus appeared to Peter and then to all the apostles, and that after that, He appeared to more than 500 brethren at one time. He also appeared to His brother, James, who later became the leader of the church in Jerusalem. Paul then reminds his readers that Jesus appeared to him, referring to his conversion experience on the road to Damascus (Acts 9:1-9).

The Overall Significance

The overwhelming significance of the resurrection of Jesus is to be seen in the fact that it is an event that sets Christianity apart from all other world religions.

The Resurrection is the unique stamp of Christianity, for only Christianity can claim an empty tomb for its founder. No resurrection has ever been claimed for Abraham, Buddha, Confucius, or Mohammed. It is no wonder that Peter claimed that "our living hope" is based on "the resurrection of Jesus Christ from the dead" (1 Peter 1:3).

I believe it was the great Bible teacher, Walter Martin (1928-1989), who once summarized the significance of the Resurrection with this observation: "The resurrection of Jesus Christ is either one of the most wicked, vicious, heartless hoaxes ever foisted upon the minds of men, or it is the most fantastic fact of history."

The Empty Tomb

Let's consider the evidence of the Resurrection, and in doing so, we must start with the fact of the empty tomb.

The Gospels tell us that Jesus was buried in the tomb of a wealthy man, Joseph of Arimathea (Matthew 27:57-60). Three days later that tomb was empty. It was empty despite the fact that it had been sealed by a huge stone weighing close to two tons and despite the fact that it had been guarded continuously by Roman soldiers (Matthew 27:62-66 and Mark 15:43-46).

The Scriptures reveal not only the careful security precautions which were taken by both the Jews and the Romans, they also reveal that the Jews did not challenge the fact that the tomb was empty. That's because the tomb was empty! They could not argue with that fact, so they manufactured a story to explain why it was empty. They paid the Roman guards of the tomb to say that Jesus' disciples had stolen his body during the night while the guards were sleeping! (Matthew 28:11-14)

Again, the tomb was empty! No one could deny that fact. Liars had to be hired to provide an explanation.

A Modern "Explanation"

What's worse is that men have been concocting silly stories ever since to try to explain away the resurrection of Jesus.

I experienced a startling explanation back in the 1980's when I ran across an Easter sermon in the *Dallas Morning News* that had been preached by a seminary professor to a group of students at a university in Dallas. He argued that the disciples' reaction to the crucifixion of Jesus was similar to what happened among the followers of Martin Luther King after his assassination.

He explained that as King's followers sat around and reminisced about his speeches and their experiences with him, he became alive in their hearts. "That's all there was to the Resurrection," he told the students. "The memory of Jesus began to burn in the hearts of His disciples as they reminisced about Him."

So the disciples of Jesus gave their lives to heart burn? Again, what total nonsense!

Other Explanations

Let's consider some of the arguments against the Resurrection that have been offered throughout history. As we do so, I think you will sense that the shallowness of the skeptics' arguments speak louder, in many respects, than the counter-arguments of Christians.[1]

1) Confusion — Perhaps the silliest argument of all is that the disciples went to the wrong tomb! Yes, some supposedly learned men have proposed this theory over the years.

Yet, the Gospel accounts tell us that Mary Magdalene and Mary, the mother of Jesus, both accompanied Joseph of Arimathea and Nicodemas to the tomb and watched them prepare the body for burial (Matthew 27:56-61 and John 19: 38-42). Are we to suppose that when the women returned they could not find their way?

And even if they did get lost and looked in the wrong tomb, did Peter and John do the same thing? Did the Roman soldiers forget which tomb they were guarding? Did Joseph of Arimathea suddenly have a memory lapse as to where his tomb was located? And why didn't the Jewish leaders simply go to the right tomb and produce the body?

The answer is simple: the tomb was empty!

2) Theft — The oldest explanation of the empty tomb is the one the Jews made up and bribed the Roman soldiers to tell — namely, that the body of Jesus was stolen by His disciples. Yes, this explanation would have us believe that Peter, Andrew, James and John were body snatchers!

Now wait a minute. Are we really to believe that a small rag-tag band of followers who were scared witless at the arrest of Jesus and who fled into the night to save their own skins, suddenly found the courage three days later to take on a guard of Roman soldiers?

Even more significant, what would have been the motivation of the disciples to steal the body? We're told over and over again in the Scriptures that they did not understand that Jesus was to be resurrected (Mark 9:30-32). Their behavior after the crucifixion testified to this as they sat around in despair mourning the loss of their leader.

And yet, this very group suddenly came alive with hope and went forth boldly proclaiming the Resurrection at the risk of their lives. Are we really to believe that a group of frightened disciples could be transformed into a courageous band of fearless proclaimers by snatching a body, hiding it, and then committing their lives to a lie? That's more difficult to believe than the Resurrection!

3) Hallucination — One of the popular modern day theories has been the idea that the disciples experienced a series of hallucinations. As one advocate of this novel concept has put it, "They experienced a disruption of the physio-chemical structures of the brain in such a way as to be able to see what they desperately wanted to see."[2]

I will grant that Mary Magdalene might have had an hallucination. After all, she was a frightened and frustrated young woman wandering around in a cemetery at day break. As a matter of fact, the reaction of the disciples to her news of the empty tomb and her encounter with angels who informed her of the Resurrection indicates that they thought she had been "seeing things" (Luke 24:11).

But what about the appearance of Jesus to all the apostles on three different occasions, or His appearance to 500 believers on a Galilean mountain, or His ascension before a host of disciples? (1 Corinthians 15:5-7 and Acts 1:1-11).

An hallucination is a highly subjective experience and a very personal one. Like beauty, it is in the eye of the beholder. To believe that 500 people could have the same hallucination simultaneously takes more faith than a belief in the Resurrection! And furthermore, the hallucination theory does not explain the empty tomb.

4) Hypnosis — Another modern theory is that the disciples experienced mass hypnosis. The advocates of this idea argue that the disciples so desperately wanted Jesus to rise from the dead that they created an aura of auto-suggestion (or mental hypnosis) and thus, whenever the name of Jesus was mentioned, His disciples believed they could see Him.

Now, mass hypnosis is a probability, with even as many as 500 people, given precisely the right type of controlled environment and the proper mass medium like radio, television, or film. But mass hypnosis without some form of mass media, and without a professional hypnotist, and without ideal conditions, is utterly outside the realm of sound reasoning.

So, I ask you, how could 500 people in the open air of a country side, before the invention of mass media, and before the discovery of hypnosis, be subject to mass hypnosis? And how does this explain the fact of the empty tomb? I think it's obvious that the skeptics are grasping at straws.

5) Fainting — This leaves us with a centuries old theory that has been resurrected and popularized by an apostate Christian named Hugh Schonfield. It's called the "swoon theory."

This is the idea that Jesus really didn't die on the cross. Instead, He just passed out and then woke up three days later. Schonfield revived this idea in 1965 in his book called *The Passover Plot*.[3]

Mr. Schonfield would ask us to believe that after Jesus was scourged and crucified, and after He had laid in a cold, damp tomb for three days without food or water, He suddenly revived, removed His burial wrappings, rolled back the stone, and ran around the country side for 40 days without the benefit of even a dose of penicillin or a tetanus shot. Only a fool could believe such utter nonsense!

6) Nostalgia — There is one other theory that has become very popular among modern day liberal theologians. It is what I call the "nostalgia theory." It's the idea I mentioned earlier that the Resurrection occurred only in the hearts of the disciples.

Such a ridiculous concept is a natural outgrowth of liberal apostasy because it leaves them with the kind of Jesus they like — one who was only human. Their "messiah" turns out to be a man who meant well, but who in reality was a deluded fool who thought he was God in the flesh.

This theory denies the well documented post-Resurrection appearances of Jesus, and like all the other theories, it fails completely to explain the fact of the empty tomb.

A Summary

The tomb of Jesus was empty. It was empty not because it was the wrong tomb. Nor was it empty because the body had been stolen.

The fact of the empty tomb was not based on hallucinations or hypnosis. It certainly was not based on daydreaming or wishful thinking. The tomb was empty! That is an historical fact.

But let me hasten to say that the greatest evidence of the resurrection of Jesus is not the empty tomb.

Powerful Evidence

The greatest evidence of the Resurrection in Scripture is to be seen in the transformed lives of Jesus' disciples. For within 50 days of His crucifixion, His disciples had been miraculously transformed from a defeated, frustrated, hopeless group of individuals into a confident band of Christian soldiers determined to win the world for their Lord.

Jesus' own brother, James, who did not believe in Him while He was alive, became the leader of the Church in Jerusalem. Peter, who denied Him three times in a fit of cowardice, began to proclaim Him boldly, even before the very Sanhedrin Council that had condemned Jesus to death (Acts 4:1-12). A young Christian by the name of Stephen gave his life for Jesus (Acts 7:51-60). And the most ruthless persecutor of the church, Saul of Tarsus, became the greatest missionary in the history of the church all because he encountered the risen Lord on the road to Damascus (Acts 9:1-9).

I ask you, what more evidence could one demand?

The Most Convincing Evidence

Well, there is more evidence, and I consider it to be the most convincing evidence of all. I have in mind the way in which people's lives continue to be transformed today through their encounter with a living Jesus.

Have you met Him? Have you been born again by placing your faith in Him? Romans 10:9 says "if you confess with your mouth Jesus as Lord, and believe in your heart that God raised Him from the dead, you shall be saved."

Salvation is to be found in a personal relationship with a living Jesus. Here's how Jesus expressed it: "This is eternal life, that they may know You, the only true God, and Jesus Christ whom You have sent" (John 17:3).

When one of Jesus' disciples named Thomas finally encountered Him after His resurrection, he cried out, "My Lord and my God!" Jesus replied, "Because you have seen Me you have believed. Blessed are those who have not seen and yet believe" (John 20:28-29). I challenge you to believe in the risen Lord, "that believing you may have life in His name" (John 20:31).

Question and Answers

1) What about the claim that the tomb of Jesus was recently discovered in Jerusalem?

In February of 2007 Oscar-winning director, James Cameron (*The Titanic*), and his counterpart, Emmy award-winning documentary film maker, Simcha Jacobovici, held a press conference in New York to promote a film they had produced for the Discovery Channel entitled *The Lost Tomb of Jesus.*[4]

Displaying some ossuaries (bone boxes) discovered in Jerusalem, they claimed that the boxes came from "the family tomb" of Jesus and that one of the boxes actually contained the bones of Jesus.

Needless to say, this announcement caused a sensation — not among the general public, but among professional archeologists. The general public seemed to yawn and dismiss the whole show as nothing but a bunch of Hollywood hype. Archeologists, on the other hand, reacted in fury. They were outraged that two amateurs who knew little or nothing about archeology would have the audacity to make such absurd claims.

You see, the discovery was nothing new. The tomb and its contents were discovered in 1980 by some construction workers who were digging a foundation for a new building in Jerusalem. The find was immediately turned over to a team of professional archeologists headed up by Professor Amos Kloner of Bar-Ilam University in Israel.

The tomb contained ten limestone ossuaries. Six of the ten had names scratched on them: Jesus the son of Joseph, Matthew, Jofa, Judah the son of Jesus, and two with the name of Mary.

Professor Kloner never made any attempt to associate this find with Jesus of Nazareth. His reasons were quite simple. First, the father of Jesus was a humble carpenter who could not have afforded a luxury crypt for his family. Second, the name of Jesus was so common among Jews in the First Century that it appears on 98 other tombs and 21 other ossuaries.

Professor Kloner responded to the claims of Cameron and

Jacobovici as "nonsense." "It makes a great story for a TV film," he said, "but it is impossible." He added:

> There is no likelihood that Jesus and his relatives had a family tomb. They were a Galilee family with no ties to Jerusalem. This tomb belonged to a middle-class family . . . I refute all their claims and efforts to waken a renewed interest in the finding. With all due respect, they are not archeologists.

There are other factors to be taken into consideration in evaluating the claims of Cameron and Jacobovici. For one thing, there is no historical record of Jesus ever being referred to by His followers as "Jesus, the son of Joseph." To His disciples He was "Jesus of Nazareth, the Son of God."

Nor did His family live in Jerusalem. Their residence was 70 miles north in the village of Nazareth, located in the Galilee of Israel. At the time Jesus was killed, He was a pilgrim in Jerusalem — thus the necessity to bury Him in a borrowed tomb, not a family tomb.

Cameron and Jacobovici tried to buttress their claim with a reference to DNA testing. But the only thing the DNA tests revealed is that some of the people buried in the tomb were related, and some were not.

Joe Zias, who was the curator for anthropology and archaeology at the Rockefeller Museum in Jerusalem from 1972 to 1997, and who personally catalogued the ossuaries, was very harsh in his evaluation of the claims made by Cameron and Jacobovici: "Simcha has no credibility whatsoever . . . He's pimping off the Bible . . . Projects like these make a mockery of the archeological profession."[5]

Perhaps the best summary quoted in the press was by Pastor Nick Stewart of the Lighthouse Free Will Baptist Church in Victoria, Texas. He said:[6]

It is ludicrous to believe this is anything more than a Hollywood attempt to malign the faith during the Easter season. It is the same tired nonsense that they tried with *The Da Vinci Code.* The thought of a righteous, risen Savior and Judge who contradicts their worldly life-style is more than they can stand.

Oh yes, there is one more point that should be made. Regardless of where the tomb of Jesus may be, we know for certain from the testimony of many eye-witnesses that it is empty. In short, no one is ever going to find the bones of Jesus.

2) If Jesus was truly resurrected, then why didn't Mary Magdalene recognize Him when she encountered a man at the tomb of Jesus who claimed to be Jesus?

This story is found in John 20:11-18. John says Mary Magdalene was standing outside the tomb weeping because the body of Jesus was missing. She was suddenly confronted by two angels who asked her why she was crying, and she answered, "Because they have taken away my Lord, and I do not know where they have laid Him." John then states that as she turned around, she "beheld Jesus standing there, and did not know that it was Jesus." Instead, she assumed He was the gardener.

There really is nothing strange at all about this story. Think of it for a moment — if you buried your best friend and then went to visit his grave the next day and he were to confront you, wouldn't you assume he was someone else? You would probably say, "Wow! You really startled me because I have a friend who looks just like you, and I attended his funeral yesterday."

Once Jesus identified Himself, and the incredible reality of His resurrection registered with Mary's mind, she had no problem recognizing Him (John 20:16-18).

Two of Jesus' disciples had the same sort of experience as they were walking to the village of Emmaus, located a few miles outside of Jerusalem. Jesus suddenly approached them and began walking with them and listening to them as they discussed His crucifixion and rumors of His resurrection. Jesus began to teach them from Moses and the Prophets about how the death and resurrection of the Messiah had been prophesied, and as He was teaching, they suddenly realized that He was none other than Jesus of Nazareth, the resurrected Lord (Luke 24:13-35).

3) Was Jesus raised bodily or as a spirit being?

True resurrection is bodily resurrection to eternal life. Jesus was raised bodily, and He emphasized this to His disciples because they were so astonished over His resurrection that they thought He was a spirit (Luke 24:36-37).

Jesus' response was to exhort them to touch and feel Him in order to determine that He was not some sort of spirit being: "See My hands and My feet, that it is I Myself; touch Me and see, for a spirit does not have flesh and bones as you see that I have" (Luke 24:39). And then, to emphasize that He was truly a material being, He asked His disciples for something to eat. They gave Him a piece of broiled fish, and He ate it in their presence (Luke 24:41-43).

What Jesus did here was very important because one of the first heresies to afflict the early Church was that of Gnosticism. The Gnostics were Gentile Christians with a Greek worldview. Since Greek philosophy taught that the material world is evil, it was impossible for a person with that viewpoint to believe that God, who is perfectly holy, could become flesh. Therefore, the Christian Gnostics taught that Jesus was a spirit being who was not incarnate in the flesh and who never truly died and was not truly resurrected.

Several passages in the New Testament are directed against this apostate teaching. One of the most important is found in 1 John 1:1 where the Apostle John wrote: "What was from the beginning, what we have heard, what we have seen with our eyes, what we beheld and our hands handled, concerning the Word of Life . . ." Notice, how John states that Jesus was seen, heard, and "handled" with their hands.

Some have assumed that Jesus' resurrection was a spiritual one rather than a physical one because His resurrection body behaved in peculiar ways. For example, when He finished teaching the two men on the road to Emmaus, He simply "vanished from their sight" (Luke 24:31). And when the two men went to Jerusalem to tell the apostles about their experience, while they were relating the story, Jesus suddenly appeared in their midst (Luke 24:35-36).

After His resurrection, Jesus seemed to appear and disappear at will. He also seemed to move about at high speed, being in Jerusalem one moment and then appearing a short time later in the Galilee (John 21:1-7).

But these unnatural characteristics of Jesus' resurrection body can be explained by the fact that His resurrection body was a glorified body, like the one believers will receive when they are resurrected.

Paul explains in 1 Corinthians 15:42-44 that our glorified bodies will be similar to the ones we have now, but also different. They will be imperishable, glorious, powerful, and spiritual — but not in the sense of being a spirit, for a spirit does not have a body. They will be spiritual in the sense that they will be completely subjected to the guidance of the Holy Spirit.

It appears that our very tangible resurrection bodies will have a different dimension to them, allowing us to do things that are not possible in our present bodies — like appear and disappear and move about at high speed. Notice that Paul says our glorified bodies will be "powerful." This same idea is implied in Philippians 3:21 where Paul wrote that when we are resurrected, Jesus "will transform the body of our humble state into conformity with the body of His glory, by the exertion of the power that He has even to subject all things to Himself."

3) Were there any prophecies that the Messiah would rise from the dead, or was the resurrection of Jesus an unexpected event? His disciples seemed to react as if His resurrection was totally unexpected.

It is true that the disciples of Jesus reacted to His resurrection as if it were a total surprise, but that was because it was such an incredulous event. It was not because they had not been told it would happen, both my the ancient Hebrew prophets and by Jesus Himself.

In Psalm 16, written one thousand years before the birth of Jesus, King David prophesied that God would not allow "His Holy One to undergo decay" (Psalm 16:10). This psalm is quoted twice in the New Testament as a prophecy about the Resurrection, once by Peter (Acts 2:30-31) and once by Paul (Acts 13:33-37).

The Resurrection is clearly implied in another psalm of David's — Psalm 22. The first 24 verses of this remarkable psalm are about the crucifixion of the Messiah. Verse 16 contains one of the most incredible of all Messianic prophecies — namely, that the Messiah would die by having His hands and feet pierced. Verses 19-21 contain a prayer of the Messiah as He is suffering in His death throes. He cries out to God for deliverance from the "lion's mouth," an obvious reference to Satan (1 Peter 5:8). Verses 22-24 contain a hymn of praise thanking God for answering the prayer, making it obvious that the Resurrection takes place between verses 21 and 22.

Isaiah 53, which is one of the greatest of Old Testament passages about the suffering and death of the Messiah, also contains verses that clearly point to His resurrection. Verse

10, for example, states that although the Messiah will "render Himself as a guilt offering, He will see His offspring [the Redeemed]," and His days will be "prolonged." The following verse repeats the promise of His resurrection by stating that "He will see the light and be satisfied."

There are also symbolic prophecies in the Hebrew Scriptures that point to the resurrection of the Messiah. One, of course, is the story of Jonah who was swallowed by a huge fish, remained within the fish for three days and three nights, and was then regurgitated back to life (Jonah 1-2). Jesus referred to this story in His teachings and used it as a prophecy of His death and resurrection: "For just as Jonah was three days and three nights in the belly of the sea monster, so shall the Son of Man be three days and three nights in the heart of the earth" (Matthew 12:38-40).

Another significant symbolic prophecy of the Resurrection that can be found in the Old Testament is the story of Abraham and Isaac. Abraham was commanded by God to sacrifice his son, Isaac, and Abraham proceeded to make the preparations, believing that God could raise his son from the dead. But the sacrificial act was interrupted when God called out to Abraham from Heaven, told him to stop, and then supplied him with a ram to offer in place of his son (Genesis 22:1-14).

In the New Testament book of Hebrews, the writer refers back to this story, saying, Abraham "considered that God is able to raise men even from the dead; from which he also received him [Isaac] back as a type" (Hebrews 11:19).

Jesus prophesied repeatedly about His death, burial and resurrection. The earliest of these prophecies occurred while He was teaching in Jerusalem during His first visit there. After Jesus had cleansed the Temple of money-changers, the Jewish leaders confronted Him about His authority to take such an action (John 2:13-18). Specifically, they asked Him for a sign of His authority. His response was, "Destroy this temple, and in three days I will raise it up" (John 2:19).

This answer perplexed the Jews. They wondered how He could reconstruct a temple in three days that had taken 46 years to build (John 2:20). But the passage relates that Jesus "was speaking of the temple of His body" (John 2:21). And it further states that after He was raised from the dead, His disciples remembered what He had said about the temple, and they realized He was speaking of His resurrection (John 2:22).

Following His transfiguration on a mountain top in the presence of Peter, James and John, Jesus ordered them not to share the experience with anyone "until the Son of Man should rise from the dead" (Mark 9:9). We are told that His disciples were puzzled by this statement and that they spent some time discussing among themselves "what rising from the dead might mean" (Mark 9:10).

After Peter's confession at Caesarea-Philippi that Jesus was "the Christ, the Son of the living God" (Matthew 16:16), we are told that Jesus "began to show His disciples that He must go to Jerusalem and suffer many things from the elders and chief priests and scribes, and be killed, and be raised up on the third day" (Matthew 16:21, Mark 9:31, and Luke 9:22).

In His Good Shepherd Discourse, recorded in John 10:1-18, Jesus proclaimed that "the Father loves Me, because I lay down My life that I may take it up again." He proceeded to state, "I have authority to lay it down, and I have authority to take it up again" (John 10:17-18).

One of the most specific statements of Jesus about His death and resurrection is contained in Matthew 20:18-20 (see also: Mark 10:33-34 and Luke 18:31-33):

> Behold, we are going up to Jerusalem, and the
> Son of Man will be delivered to the chief
> priests and scribes, and they will condemn
> Him to death, and will deliver Him to the
> Gentiles to mock and scourge and crucify
> Him, and on the third day, He will be raised
> up.

At His last supper with His disciples, Jesus made a start-ling prophecy: "You will all fall away because of Me this night" (Matthew 26:31). He stated this desertion would occur to fulfill a prophecy in Zechariah 13:7 that when the Shep-herd is struck down, the sheep will scatter. He then added, "But after I have been raised, I will go before you to Galilee" (Matthew 26:32 and Mark 14:27-28).

The Scriptures state that the disciples of Jesus did not understand these statements about the Messiah's resurrection, but they were afraid to ask Jesus for an explanation (Mark 9:32, Luke 9:45 and John 16:15-22). In fact, the Scriptures say that the meaning of these resurrection prophecies was "concealed from them so that they might not perceive it" (Luke 9:45).

It was only after His resurrection that the disciples of Jesus had their eyes opened. The prophecies were brought to their remembrance by the Holy Spirit, and they began to comprehend that Jesus meant exactly what He had said. All of which was in fulfillment of a prophecy of Jesus when He said, "the Helper, the Holy Spirit, whom the Father will send in My name, He will teach you all things, and bring to your remembrance all that I have said to you" (John 14:26).

All these quotations from both the Old and New Testa-ments should make it clear that the resurrection of Jesus was no johnny-come-lately concept that was conjured up by the disciples of Jesus after His death.

4) Do Muslims believe in the death, burial and resurrection of Jesus?

No. They believe Jesus was a great prophet, but not as great as Mohammed. They deny that He was ever crucified or that He was resurrected (Sura 4:157). The Quran states, instead, that He was taken up to Heaven without dying (Sura 4:158). By denying Jesus' death, burial and resurrection, Muslims are actually blasphemers of Him.

5) Can a person be a Christian who denies the Resurrection?

No! A belief in the resurrection of Jesus is an essential element of the Gospel that must be believed in order for a person to be born again and sealed by the Holy Spirit for redemption (1 Corinthians 15:1-4, 14, 17).

OZYMANDIAS

A Poem by Percy Bysshe Shelley

I met a traveller from an antique land
Who said: Two vast and trunkless legs of stone
Stand in the desert. Near them, on the sand,
Half sunk, a shattered visage lies, whose frown
And wrinkled lip, and sneer of cold command
Tell that its sculptor well those passions read
Which yet survive, stamped on these lifeless things,
The hand that mocked them and the heart that fed.
And on the pedestal these words appear:
"My name is Ozymandias, king of kings:
Look on my works, ye Mighty, and despair!"
Nothing beside remains. Round the decay
Of that colossal wreck, boundless and bare
The lone and level sands stretch far away.

This powerful and insightful poem was written in 1818 by Shelley in response to the arrival in London of the remains of a colossal statue of Ramesses the Great, Pharaoh of the 19th Dynasty of Egypt. Ozymandias was another name for Ramesses. The statue actually featured an inscription that read: "King of kings am I, Ozymandias. If anyone would know how great I am and where I lie, let him surpass my works."

"Vanity of vanity! All is vanity." — King Solomon in Ecclesiastes 1:2.

"When the game is over, the king and the pawn go into the same box." — Italian proverb.

Chapter 7

Are You Living With
An Eternal Perspective?

One of the greatest public servants in the history of England was William Gladstone (1809 - 1898) who served as Prime Minister four times during the latter half of the 19th Century.

Gladstone was a committed Christian who always attended church. (By contrast, Prime Minister Tony Blair was the only British leader in the 20th Century who regularly attended church services.) Gladstone also taught a Sunday School class throughout his adult life. In fact, his aim early in his life was to become an Anglican clergyman, but after his graduation from Oxford, his strong-willed father insisted that he enter politics.[1]

Shortly before he died, Gladstone gave a speech in which he told about being visited by an ambitious young man who sought his advice about life. The lad told the elder statesman that he admired him more than anyone living and wanted to seek his advice regarding his career.[2]

A Remarkable Interview

"What do you hope to do when you graduate from college?" Gladstone asked.

The young man replied, "I hope to attend law school, sir, just as you did."

"That's a noble goal," said Gladstone, "Then what?"

"I hope to practice law and make a good name for myself defending the poor and the outcasts of society, just as you did."

"That's a noble purpose," replied Gladstone. "Then what?"

"Well, sir, I hope one day to stand for Parliament and become a servant of the people, even as you did."

"That too is a noble hope. What then?" asked Gladstone.

"I would hope to be able to serve in the Parliament with great distinction, evidencing integrity and a concern for justice — even as you did."

"What then?" asked Gladstone.

"I would hope to serve the government as Prime Minister with the same vigor, dedication, vision, and integrity as you did."

"And what then?" asked Gladstone.

"I would hope to retire with honors and write my memoirs — even as you are presently doing — so that others could learn from my mistakes and triumphs."

"All of that is very noble," said Gladstone, "and then what?"

The young man thought for a moment. "Well, sir, I suppose I will then die."

"That's correct," said Gladstone. "And then what?"

The young man looked puzzled. "Well, sir," he answered hesitantly, "I've never given that any thought."

"Young man," Gladstone responded, "the only advice I have for you is for you to go home, read your Bible, and *think about eternity.*"

Good Advice

Think about eternity! What good advice. Life goes by so quickly. It is like a vapor that is here one moment and evaporates the next. We are preparing for eternity. Are you ready?

Or, are you living like you expect to live forever? Are you focused on this life, determined to accumulate all the money, power and fame you possibly can? Are you like the young man who visited Gladstone — are you a person who has never given eternity a thought? If so, the Word of God has a stern warning for you (James 4:13-15):[3]

> And now I have a word for you who brashly announce, "Today — at the latest, tomorrow — we're off to such and such a city for the year. We're going to start a business and make a lot of money."
>
> You don't know the first thing about tomorrow. You're nothing but a wisp of fog, catching a brief bit of sun before disappearing.
>
> Instead, make it a habit to say, "If the Master wills it and we're still alive, we'll do this or that."

The Fleeting Nature of Life

This passage always reminds me of an incident that occurred in my life several years ago. A dear friend of mine whom I had taught with in a Texas college called me one day and told me he had been diagnosed with prostate cancer.

"The doctor has given me only six months to live," he reported.

I told him I was very sorry to hear the news, and I promised to pray for him and his family. Then, I added, "But keep in mind, I may be dead before you."

"Oh? Do you have cancer too?" he asked.

"No," I responded, "it's just that I do not have the promise of even one day of life, much less six months."

We all tend to live like we are going to live forever, when the fact is that we are all mortal and can die at any moment from a thousand different causes, natural or accidental. Ironically, the Bible tells us that we are to live like we are going to live forever — but not on this earth. We are to live in preparation for eternity, hopefully an eternity with God.

Most likely you are a born-again believer who has given serious thought to eternity, but who finds it difficult to maintain an eternal perspective. You repeatedly find yourself caught up with the problems of life, and the result is stress, anxiety, and even depression.

Living with an eternal perspective is one of the keys to living as an overcomer. It is a virtue that is going to become increasingly important as society continues to disintegrate and Christians come under increasing attack.

What is the secret to maintaining an eternal perspective? Much of the answer lies in your attitude about this world.

Your Attitude Toward the World

Stop for a moment and think. What is your attitude about this world? Are you enthusiastic about it? Or do you feel uncomfortable with it? Do you love the world? Or do you often feel alienated from it? Are you at home in this world? Or do you feel like a stranger?

There's an old Negro spiritual song that always challenges me to examine my attitude toward the world. The first verse goes as follows:[4]

> This world is not my home,
> I'm just a passing through.

My treasures are laid up
Somewhere beyond the blue.

The angels beckon me
From heaven's open door,
And I can't feel at home
In this world anymore.

Do those words express your feeling about this world? What word would you use to summarize your feeling? Zealous? Anxious? Enamored? Estranged? Are you comfortable or do you feel ill-at-ease?

My Attitude

Let me ask your indulgence for a moment as I share my personal feeling about this world. The word I would use is "hate." Yes, I hate this world. I hate it with a passion so strong and so intense that I find it difficult to express in words.

Now, let me hasten to clarify my feeling by stating that I do not hate God's beautiful and marvelous creation. I have been privileged to marvel over the majesty of the Alps. I have been awed by the rugged beauty of Alaska. I never cease to be amazed by the creative wonders of God in the great American Southwest. I have been blessed to see the incredible beauty of Cape Town, South Africa. And I have been overwhelmed time and time again by the stark and almost mystical bareness of the Judean wilderness in Israel.

When I say that I "hate" this world, I'm not speaking of God's creation. I'm speaking, instead, of the evil world system that we live in. Let me give you some examples of what I'm talking about:

- I hate a world where thousands of babies are murdered every day in their mother's wombs.

- I hate a world where young people in the prime of life

have their lives destroyed by illicit drugs.

- I hate a world that coddles criminals and makes a mockery of justice.

- I hate a world that glorifies crime in its movies and television programs.

- I hate a world that applauds indecent and vulgar performers like Madonna and Lady Gaga.

- I hate a world where government tries to convert gambling from a vice to a virtue.

- I hate a world in which professional athletes are paid millions of dollars a year while hundreds of thousands sleep homeless in the streets every night.

- I hate a world where people judge and condemn one another on the basis of skin color.

- I hate a world that calls evil good by demanding that homosexuality be recognized as a legitimate, alternative lifestyle.

- I hate a world in which mothers are forced to work while their children grow up in impersonal day care centers.

- I hate a world in which people die agonizing deaths from diseases like cancer and AIDS.

- I hate a world where families are torn apart by alcohol abuse.

- I hate a world where every night I see reports on the television news of child abuse, muggings, kidnaping, murders, terrorism, wars, and rumors of wars.

- I hate a world that uses the name of my God, Jesus, as a curse word.

I hope you understand now what I mean when I say, "I

hate this world!"

Jesus' Viewpoint

But how I personally feel about this world is not important. The crucial point for you to consider is the biblical view. Let's look at it, and as we do so, compare the biblical view with your own.

Let's begin with the viewpoint that Jesus told us we should have. It is recorded in John 12:25 — "He who loves his life loses it, and he who hates his life in this world shall keep it to life eternal."

Those are strong words. They are the kind that cause us to wince and think, "Surely He didn't mean what He said." But the context indicates that Jesus meant exactly what He said. So, what about it? Do you hate your life in this world or do you love it?

The Viewpoint of the Apostles

The Apostle Paul gave a very strong warning about getting comfortable with the world. In Romans 12:2 he wrote: "Do not be conformed to this world, but be transformed by the renewing of your mind." How do you measure up to this exhortation?

Are you conformed to the world? Have you adopted the world's way of dress? What about the world's way of speech or the world's love of money? Are your goals the goals of the world — power, success, fame, and riches?

The brother of Jesus expressed the matter in very pointed language. He said, "Do you not know that friendship with the world is hostility toward God? Therefore, whoever wishes to be a friend of the world makes himself an enemy of God" (James 4:4).

Are you a friend of the world? Are you comfortable with what the world has to offer in music, movies, television programs and best selling books? Friendship with the world is hostility toward God!

In fact, James puts it even stronger than that, for at the beginning of the passage I previously quoted (James 4:4), he says that those who are friendly with the world are spiritual adulterers.

The apostle John makes the same point just as strongly in 1 John 2:15-16:

> Do not love the world, nor the things in the world. If anyone loves the world, the love of the Father is not in him. For all that is in the world, the lust of the flesh, and the lust of the eyes, and the boastful pride of life, is not from the Father, but is from the world.

There is no way to escape the sobering reality of these words. Do you love the world? If so, the love of the Father is not in you!

The Focus of Your Mind

Paul tells us how to guard against becoming comfortable with the world. In Colossians 3:2 he says, "Set your mind on the things above, not on the things that are on earth." In Philippians 4:8 he expresses the same admonition in these words:

> Finally, brethren, whatever is true, whatever is honorable, whatever is right, whatever is pure, whatever is lovely, whatever is of good repute, if there is any excellence and if anything worthy of praise, let your mind dwell on these things.

As these verses indicate, one of the keys to living a triumphant life in Christ — to living a joyous and victorious life in the midst of a world wallowing in despair — is to live with a conscious eternal perspective.

What does that mean? In the words of Peter, that means living as "aliens and strangers" in this world (1 Peter 2:11). Similarly, in the words of the writer of Hebrews, it means living as "strangers and exiles." (Hebrews 11:13). Paul put it this way: "Do not set your minds on earthly things, for our citizenship is in heaven" (Philippians 3:19-20).

The great Christian writer, C. S. Lewis, explained that to live with an eternal perspective means "living as commandos operating behind the enemy lines, preparing the way for the coming of the Commander-in-Chief."[5]

A Biblical Example

There is a powerful biblical example of what can happen when a believer gets his eyes off the Lord and starts focusing on transient things rather than eternal matters. It is found in Psalm 73.

All students of the Bible are familiar with Psalm 51 in which David confessed his sin of adultery with Bathsheba. But few seem to be aware of Psalm 73 which contains the confession of David's worship leader, Asaph.

In this remarkable psalm, Asaph confesses that he almost lost his faith when he lost his eternal perspective. It happened when he did something that all of us tend to do from time to time —namely, he took his eyes off the Lord and put them instead on the wicked. When he did so, he noticed the prosperity of the wicked and began to wonder if his devotion to God was really worth the effort (Psalm 73:1-3).

Has that ever happened to you? Surely it has. I think it has happened to all of us from time to time.

Struggling with the Prosperity of the Wicked

It's the end of the month, and the bills are due. You're sitting at your desk writing check after check. Suddenly, you reach that minimum balance you must maintain in order to pay the daily bills of the new month — food, gasoline, clothing, repairs, etc. But you still have a stack of bills to pay! You sigh in exasperation, wondering when you will ever be able to catch up with what you owe.

As you sit there staring dejectedly at your meager balance, you begin to think about a friend of yours at work. He is a vain and profane man, with a mouth like a sewer. He could care less about God. He is unfaithful to his wife. He ignores his children. He is consumed with sports and gambles constantly. Yet, he never seems to have a worry. He lives in a beautiful house, drives a fancy car, and eats at the finest restaurants.

Your heart begins to fill with envy and anger. You feel like crying out, "Lord, I serve You faithfully, and all I ever seem to get in return is trouble. My colleague at work is a complete reprobate, and he doesn't seem to have a worry in the world! What's wrong? Am I spinning my wheels with You? Is my tithe a waste of my money? Is my faithfulness of no concern to You? The way things are going, I might as well serve the devil and get some enjoyment out of life!"

Sound familiar? Well, this is exactly what happened to Asaph. He lost his eternal perspective, got his eyes on the wicked, and started wallowing in self-pity (Psalm 73:2-3).

Asaph's Sin

It's amazing how irrational we become when we allow self-pity to take over our thinking. When it happened to Asaph, he started fantasizing about the rich. He began to tell himself that they are "always at ease," always increasing in wealth, never facing the problems of other people (Psalm 73:4-5,12). All of which, of course, is utter nonsense. In fact, the opposite is true. The rich often tend to have far more problems than other people. For one thing, they must constantly be concerned about their money — how to protect it and multiply it.

It was while Asaph was caught up in this fantasy world that he committed a grievous sin against God. He blasphemed the love and faithfulness of God by exclaiming: "Surely in vain I have kept my heart pure and washed my hands in innocence; for I have been stricken all day long and chastened every morning" (Psalm 73:13-14).

Asaph's Turning Point

Asaph was literally on the verge of losing his faith. His spirit was in turmoil. He was wrestling with monstrous doubt. The wrestling match continued "until I came into the sanctuary of God; then I perceived their end [the end of the wicked]" (Psalm 73:17).

Asaph is maddeningly vague at this point. He does not tell us what happened to him when he went to the Lord's house, except that his eternal perspective was restored. Was it a song that touched his heart? Could it have been a scripture reading or a sermon? Perhaps it was a word of encouragement from a discerning friend. It might even have been a death in his family. We just don't know. All we know for sure is that something touched his heart and reminded him of the eternal destiny of the wicked.

He states that he was reminded that the wicked walk in "slippery places" and that God may cause them to be cast down at any moment, being swept away by "sudden terror" (Psalm 73:8-19). In other words, Asaph was reminded that life is very tentative — here one moment and gone the next.

The Impact of Death

I think this is the reason that the death of Princess Diana had such an enormous impact on the world. Here was a woman who had it all — everything the world dreams of having. She had beauty, charm, wealth, fame, and influence. She had the "good life." Yet, in one terrifying moment, it all disappeared. She was reduced to equality with all of us — a mortal person gone to meet her Creator.

It was a sobering event. It drove home the transitory nature of life. I'm sure it caused many people to pause and think about eternity for the first time in their lives.

As I have pointed out repeatedly in this book, the Bible says that most people live in life-long fear of death. In fact, the Bible puts it even stronger than that. It says that most people live in "slavery" to the fear of death (Hebrews 2:15). This is the reason that a death in the family, or the death of a friend or a celebrity, always has such an impact. It reminds us of our mortality, and it triggers our eternal perspective.

A Personal Experience with Death

I had an experience with death many years ago that I will never forget. It emphasized to me the fragility of life and the inevitability of eternity. It also impacted me with the importance of keeping my priorities in order at all times.

The setting was the Cajun country of Southern Louisiana. I was holding a meeting at a fairly large church in Jennings, Louisiana. Following the Sunday evening service, I went to the door to greet people as they left. A young woman about 30 years old came up to me and enthusiastically thanked me for the message. She said she could hardly wait for the Monday evening service. I was speaking on the "Signs of the Times" that point to the soon return of Jesus. The Sunday message had caught her imagination, and she was excited.

"I have so many questions," she said, "but I'll have to hold them till later because I've got to rush to my job."

"Oh?" I responded. "What kind of job do you have on Sunday evening?"

"I run the skating rink," she answered, "and we've got a lot of church kids coming over to skate this evening. I've got to hurry and get the place opened."

I thanked her for her kind comments and urged her not to forget her questions. She left hurriedly.

A Shocking Call

About 10:30 that evening the phone rang at the house where I was staying. I heard my host, one of the congregation's elders, suddenly exclaim, "Oh no! Oh no!" He hung up the phone and yelled at me, "Get your coat. We've got to go to the hospital."

As we tore across town in his truck, he explained that the call had been about the young woman who managed the skating rink. She had been skating with the kids when she suddenly dropped to the floor. She had been rushed to the hospital. The situation looked critical.

The moment we walked into the hospital lobby, we knew she was dead. Groups of youngsters and friends from the church were gathered in small groups all over the lobby and down the main hallway. Some were praying. Some were singing softly. Some were just comforting one another with hugs of reassurance.

She had suffered a massive cerebral hemorrhage. She was only 32. Death had come instantaneously. The doctor said she was probably dead before she hit the floor.

Reacting in the Lord

Her older sister arrived and was given the terrible news. She was known as a woman of great faith. We tried to console her but she kept consoling us, reminding us that her sister was now with the Lord. She went from group to group encouraging them with the victory her sister now enjoyed.

Then her brother arrived. He was a man of the world. He had treated his sisters harshly because of their religious convictions.

When he learned of his sister's death, he was overcome

with grief and guilt. He fell to the floor in a clump and began to weep and moan loudly.

His sister rushed to him, grabbed him by the shoulders and literally lifted him off the floor. She slammed him up against the wall and held him there with her forearm. Looking directly into his eyes, she said, "Don't weep for your sister. Weep for yourself. She's in Heaven with the Lord. But if that were you in there on that table, you would be in Hell!"

I was taken aback by what appeared to be a brutal approach to a grieving person. But it must have had the right impact because within a year that brother had accepted the Lord.

Reacting Outside the Lord

I started moving up and down the hallway from group to group, praying with them and trying as best as I knew how to offer some consoling words. Suddenly, a side door flew open and in came two paramedics running and pushing a litter on wheels. On the stretcher was a man who looked to be 60. He was dressed in a tuxedo. They wheeled him into an emergency room.

A few minutes later a large entourage of "beautiful people" arrived, all dressed in tuxedos and evening gowns. They gathered outside the emergency room doors and waited for some word. I learned they had been partying at a night club and that the man had collapsed on the dance floor. They thought he had suffered a heart attack.

They were right. The doctor stepped into the hallway and delivered the grim news. The man was dead from a heart attack. They all stood there for a moment in a daze, and then they turned on each other like a pack of wild animals.

A daughter, dressed in a red evening dress, turned to an older woman and began to shout curses at her. The woman was her mother, the widow of the man who had just died.

There was no consolation from daughter to mother. Only curses and accusations.

"It's all your fault," the daughter screamed. "You're the cause of his heart attack. You've never given him anything but grief."

"Look who's talking," the mother shouted back, "the biggest slut in Southern Louisiana." It was a horrible scene. Family members cursing and blaming each other.

A Startling Contrast

I was standing at a corner of the hallway. Down one corridor I saw people cursing and clawing at each other. Down the other corridor I saw people consoling and loving one another. I saw death down one hallway. I saw life down the other. I saw the glory of dying in the Lord, and I saw the grim reality of dying with no hope.

Such an experience can jolt you out of your rut. It can grab you by the throat and turn you every way but loose. It certainly can force you to think about eternity.

I suspect that Asaph had some similar experience that propelled him to the Lord's house and compelled him to get his eyes back on the Lord. I think it is interesting to note that once his eternal perspective was restored, he looked back on his combat with doubt and marveled over how stupid he had been. He concluded that he was as "senseless and ignorant" as a beast (Psalm 73:21-22).

Asaph's Faith Restored

Asaph wrapped up his psalm by praising the Lord for His faithfulness in words reminiscent of Paul when he wrote, "If we are faithless, He remains faithful; for He cannot deny Himself" (2 Timothy 2:13).

Asaph expressed his restored priorities in memorable words (Psalm 73:25-28):

Whom have I in heaven but You? And besides You, I desire nothing on earth. My flesh and my heart fail, But God is the strength of my heart and my portion forever. For, behold, those who are far from You will perish; You have destroyed all those who are unfaithful to You. But as me, the nearness of God is my good; I have made the Lord God my refuge, That I may tell of all Your works.

The solution to Asaph's spiritual agony was the restoration of his eternal perspective. He was reminded that this life is fleeting, and a day of judgment is coming. He realized that he may never see justice in this life, but one day justice will prevail. He realized that he had been called to live by faith and not by sight.

Another Test of Attitude

Let me give you one last test for determining whether or not you are living with an eternal perspective: How do you feel about the Lord's return? This is an acid test that will determine whether you are in love with the world or the Lord.

The attitude of the person who is in love with the world can best be expressed in these words: "I want the Lord to return, but . . ." There is always a "but."

- "I want the Lord to return, but I want Him to come after I have made a million dollars."

- "I want the Lord to come, but I want Him to come after I've written a great novel."

- "I want the Lord to come, but I want Him to come after I've made the cover of *Time*."

- "I want the Lord to come, but I want Him to come after I've built a great church."

- "I want the Lord to come, but I want Him to come

after I'm 85 years old and have experienced all that life has to offer."

What these people are really saying is, "I want Jesus to come, but I don't want Him messing up my life!" They are in love with the world.

You see, when you are in love with someone, you want to be with them. That's a fact of life. Watch people who have just fallen in love. They want to be with each other all the time. When they are apart, they are constantly on the phone talking about when they will be together again!

The same is true of the Lord. If you truly love Jesus, you will want to be with Him. You will talk with Him in prayer. You will fellowship with Him in His Word and in worship. But these forms of communication will never satisfy your longing to be in His presence, to have personal, intimate fellowship with Him, face to face.

The Biblical Attitude

You will be like Paul, willing to stay on in this world serving the Lord, but yearning for the day when you will be united with Him, either through death or His return (2 Corinthians 5:8 and Philippians 1:23-24).

A sense of yearning is characteristic of those who live with an eternal perspective. It can be found expressed throughout the Bible —

> The patriarch Job stated that he looked forward to the day when his Redeemer would stand upon the earth because he knew that when that happened, he, Job, would receive a new body and would see the Lord. He added that the very thought was enough to cause him to faint! (Job 19:25-27)

> Abraham "lived as an alien in the land of promise" because he yearned for "the city which has founda-

tions, whose architect and builder is God" (Hebrews 11:9-10).

Moses thought it was better to be ill-treated for the promised Messiah's sake than to own all the riches of Egypt because he was looking forward to his heavenly reward (Hebrews 11:26).

David relished the promise of God that one day He will send His Son to terrify the nations with His wrath and reign as King on Mt. Zion (Psalm 2:5-6).

Isaiah's heart was so filled with desire to be with the Lord that he cried out, "Oh, that You would rend the heavens and come on down . . . to make Your name known to Your adversaries, that the nations may tremble at Your presence!" (Isaiah 64:1-2).

Jeremiah dreamed of when the Lord would "roar from on high, and utter His voice from His holy habitation" (Jeremiah 25:30).

Ezekiel spent nine chapters (40-48) describing in detail the glorious Millennial Temple of the Lord, obviously yearning for the day it would be built. He concluded the description with the reason for his yearning. He revealed that the city will have a new name: "Yahweh Shammah," which means, "The Lord is there" (Ezekiel 48:35).

Daniel had visions about the Lord returning to reign over all the earth, together with His saints (Daniel 7:13-14,18,27).

Micah cried out for the day when the Lord will dwell once again in Jerusalem and will "teach us about His ways" and "we will walk in His paths" (Micah 4:2).

The Old Testament ends with Malachi looking forward to the day when the "sun of righteousness will rise with healing in its wings." He says his response will be to "go forth and skip about" like a calf released from a stall! (Malachi 4:2).

This yearning to be with the Lord continues throughout the New Testament. Peter exhorted us to live with our hope fixed confidently on the return of Jesus (1 Peter 1:13-16).

Paul urged us to live with the love of the Lord's appearing in our hearts (2 Timothy 4:8). He also told the Church to pray, "Maranatha!" meaning, "Our Lord come!" (1 Corinthians 16:22).

The New Testament ends with the words of John crying out, "Amen. Come Lord Jesus!" (Revelation 22:20).

From beginning to end, we find people throughout the Scriptures who are in love with God and who are expressing that love by yearning to be with Him.

In contrast, we find the Church of the 21st Century yawning about the Lord's return. We are the church of Laodicea: penetrated by the world, rich and in need of nothing — not even the Lord Himself, who stands at the door knocking, asking to be let in (Revelation 3:14-17). Like that church, we are "neither cold nor hot." We are lukewarm. And the result is that we are apathetic and worldly. We desperately need to have our eternal perspective restored.

A Practical Suggestion

I suggest that the next time you let your eternal perspective slip, remember Psalm 73 and read it. When you finish, reverse the numbers and go to Psalm 37. There you will find a powerful summary of what Asaph learned. It is a psalm of Asaph's mentor, King David.

David says, "Do not fret because of evildoers . . . for they will wither quickly like the grass and fade like the green herb" (verses 1-2). He tells us what to do instead: "Trust in the Lord, and do good . . . delight yourself in the Lord" (verses 3-4). Over and over again he warns us not to fret over evildoers, for he says the day will come when they will be "cut off" (verse 9). In contrast, "those who wait upon the Lord" shall "inherit the earth" (verse 9).

What is Your Attitude?

Are you focused on this world? Are you attached to it, or do you have a sense of the fact that you are only passing through, heading for an eternal home?

This life is transitory. This life is only a prelude to eternity. The song writer, Tillit S. Teddlie put it all in perspective when he wrote:[6]

> Earth holds no treasures
> But perish with using,
> However precious they be;
> Yet there's a country
> To which I am going:
> Heaven holds all to me.

> Why should I long
> For the world with its sorrows,
> When in that home o'er the sea,
> Millions are singing
> The wonderful story?
> Heaven holds all to me.

> Heaven holds all to me,
> Brighter its glory will be;
> Joy without measure
> Will be my treasure:
> Heaven holds all to me.

There is a more contemporary song that sums up the whole essence of what it means to live with an eternal perspective:[7]

> Turn your eyes upon Jesus,
> Look full in His wonderful face,
> And the things of earth
> Will grow strangely dim
> In the light of His glory and grace.

A number of years ago I was given the blessing of meeting a great man of God named Leonard Ravenhill, a prophetic preacher from England. After our meeting, we corresponded briefly. Right before he died, in the last letter he sent me, he enclosed a small card containing a brief, one sentence message. He urged me to memorize the message and live it daily.

That was July of 1988. I still have the card. It is worn and tattered because I have made it a point to keep it in my shirt pocket at all times. The message printed on it is simple but profound: "Lord, keep me eternity conscious."

Questions and Answers

1) Does living with an eternal perspective mean that I should stop being concerned about social problems like abortion and homosexuality?

Not at all! We are not to withdraw from the world. We are to be in the world, but not of the world (John 17:11, 14-16).

Jesus called us to be "light" and "salt" in the world (Matthew 5:13-16). If we do not stand up and speak out against the evils of this world, no one will.

But we are never to fall into the deception that the answer to the world's problems is political action. The only hope for the world is the Gospel. Thus, we are to keep our priorities in order — first, to share the Gospel, and second, to speak out against the evils of society and to work to correct social injustice.

God is very concerned about justice (Isaiah 30:18 and

Micah 6:8). He often expresses His concern for widows and orphans (Psalm 68:5 and James 1:27), and He condemns those who would take advantage of them (Psalm 82:3-4). He also condemns those who are willing to pervert justice for a bribe (2 Chronicles 19:7).

But He is even more concerned about the salvation of souls. He sent His Son to die for our sins so that we can be reconciled to Him. He does not wish that any should perish, but that all might come to repentance and be saved (2 Peter 3:9).

The classic error of those who have given their allegiance to the Social Gospel is that they are more concerned about people's current physical well being than their eternal destiny. We should be concerned about both, but the priority must be given to the person's eternal well being.

Be concerned about feeding and housing the poor and the homeless, but be more concerned about sharing the Gospel with them as their physical needs are being attended to.

The basic error of the Social Gospel advocates is that they end up loving people into Hell.

2) What are some practical ways of keeping an eternal perspective?

One of the most important is to constantly review your priorities. What is first in your life? Is it money? Power? Fame? Family? Career?

Your first priority should always be your relationship with God. Your family should come second. Your career must be kept in third place.

Maintaining these priorities in their proper order is a daily struggle. Staying in the Word and devoting all aspects of your life to prayer through a daily devotional time is one of the keys to maintaining your priorities in their proper order.

Another helpful thing to do is to seek out an accountability partner — a fellow believer who can meet with you regularly and with whom you can share the intimate details of your life. You can hold each other responsible for keeping your priorities in order while serving to encourage each other.

It is so easy to get our eyes off the Lord and focused on ourselves. That's why I have been so impressed with the "I am second" campaign that features video testimonies by celebrities who tell how they maintain the proper balance in their lives by constantly reminding themselves that they are second, and God is first.[8]

THANANTOPSIS

A Poem by William Cullen Bryant

So live, that when thy summons comes to join
The innumerable caravan which moves
To that mysterious realm where each shall take
His chamber in the silent halls of death,
Thou go not, like the quarry-slave at night,
Scourged by his dungeon; but, sustained and soothed
By an unfaltering trust, approach thy grave,
Like one who wraps the drapery of his couch
About him, and lies down to pleasant dreams.

This is the last stanza of a poem written by Bryant in 1811 when he was only 17 years old! The title is Greek for "Meditation upon Death."

William Cullen Bryant (1794-1878) was born in Massachusetts. He studied law and was admitted to the bar in 1815. He continued to write poetry and by 1832 he had won recognition as America's leading poet. Meanwhile, he had grown disillusioned with the practice of law and began working as an editor in 1825, eventually ending up as the editor of the *New York Evening Post.* He served in that capacity for over 50 years (1828-1878). In his last decade, Bryant shifted from writing poetry to translating the works of Homer.

Postscript

I want to leave you with two insightful and inspiring stories about death.

The first is an apocryphal one that has circulated on the Internet for several years. The second is a true story about a woman facing death.

The Apocryphal Story

An elderly lady with terminal cancer phoned her pastor and asked him to come to her house to help her plan her funeral.

After discussing the order of the service and the songs she wanted sung, the pastor asked her what kind of message she wanted him to deliver.

She thought for a moment and then said, "Why don't you relate the message to the fact that I have asked my children to make certain that I am buried with a fork in my right hand."

The pastor was surprised and puzzled by her statement. "Why a fork?" he asked.

"Well," she replied, "all my life I have been going to church luncheons and suppers, and I have noticed that when I finish my meal, someone always would pick up my plate and then say, 'Keep your fork because the best is yet to come.' And that's the way I feel about dying — the best is yet to come!"

The True Story[1]

The name Grace Rice MacMullen will not be familiar to most of you. She was the oldest daughter of the late evangelist John R. Rice. Grace was a vibrant, active Christian who led many people to the Lord.

Her story is all too familiar. The doctors discovered cancer, treated it with chemotherapy and she went into remission. Then the disease came back in force. The doctors told her she would have four to six months to live. That was on August 18, 1981. She went home and figured up four months and then wrote the following words:

What will I be doing on December 18?

Well, that depends. I'll be praising the Lord for His glory and goodness either by faith or by sight. If by faith, as I've been doing, my praise may be subdued, alternating with a tear at times.

If not by faith, ah then, ah then! With angels and trumpets and choirs and instruments indescribable!

I'll still be loving the Lord — maybe blindly, hesitantly, but full-heartedly, trustingly!

Or else — or else! I'll be loving him in a burst of light where shadows are washed away, to know as I am known — with that full-pouring effusion that can only at last express my stunted, limited, longing love — in purest, shimmering light and color and substance.

I shall, that day, talk to God a bit, as usual, about the things I'm thinking about, about the people I love, about how the day is going, about what I need and want.

Or yet — or yet — I shall that day talk to God! Himself, in person, no dark glass between, nor childish me to speak of childish things.

I shall on that day lie in bed, or move about with wheeled chair, finding my needs met minute-by-minute by loving hands and smiling faces.

Or, indeed, indeed! I shall be doing handsprings, cart-wheels, and run a dozen miles! To move with God's own planned grace, as Eve did; roll down a long grassy field, jump across a stream. I shall observe with undimmed eyes and hear with unstopped ears, taste with untainted buds and sniff the fragrances of another world.

Where shall I be?

Here or there?

How little it matters!

* * * * * * * * * *

Grace never made it to December 18. Death came on October 24. Her marvelous words tell us all we need to know about Christian faith in the face of death. Let me leave you with a simple question: Is that the kind of faith you have? Are you ready to die, and do you know where you will go when you die? What will be your eternal destiny? Heaven or Hell?

God of the Living

A Poem by John Ellerton

God of the living, in whose eyes
Unveiled Thy whole creation lies,
All souls are Thine; we must not say
That those are dead who pass away,
From this our world of flesh set free;
We know them living unto Thee.

Released from earthly toil and strife,
With Thee is hidden still their life;
Thine are their thoughts, their works, their powers,
All thine, and yet most truly ours,
For well we know, where'er they be,
Our dead are living unto Thee.

Not spilt like water on the ground,
Not wrapped in dreamless sleep profound,
Not wandering in unknown despair
Beyond Thy voice, Thine arm, Thy care;
Not left to lie like fallen tree;
Not dead, but living unto Thee.

Thy word is true, Thy will is just;
To Thee we leave them, Lord, in trust;
And bless Thee for the love which gave
Thy Son to fill a human grave,
That none might fear that world to see
Where all are living unto Thee.

O Breather into man of breath,
O Holder of the keys of death,
O Giver of the life within,
Save us from death, the death of sin;
That body, soul, and spirit be
For ever living unto Thee!

References

Introduction: The Fear of Death

1) Dennis Pollock, "Live Forever!" *Lamplighter* magazine published by Lamb & Lion Ministries, May-June 2003, pp. 7-9.

2) Wikipedia, "Ted Williams," http://en.wikipedia.org/wiki/Ted_Williams.

3) Quote DB, "Woody Allen Quotes," www.quotedb.com/quotes/2144.

4) BibleStudy.org, "Life Span of Biblical Patriarchs before and after Noah's Flood," http://www.biblestudy.org/maps/life-span-of-Bible-patriarchs-before-after-the-flood.html.

5) Wikipedia, "Life Expectancy," http://en.wikipedia.org/wiki/Life_expectancy.

6) Wikipedia, "World Population," http://en.wikipedia.org/wiki/World_population. See also: Lambert Dolphin, "World Population Since Creation," http://ldolphin.org/popul.html.

7) Infoplease, "Medical Advances Timeline," www.infoplease.com/ipa/A0932661.html.

8) Nobelprize.com, "Sir Alexander Fleming," http://nobelprize.org/nobel_prizes/medicine/laureates/1945/fleming-bio.html.

9) Wikipedia, "Frederic Remington," http://en.wikipedia.org/wiki/Frederic_Remington.

10) David McCullough, *Truman* (New York: Simon & Schuster, 1992), pp. 94-96.

11) Infoplease, "Life Expectancy by Age, 1850–2004," http://www.infoplease.com/ipa/A0005140.html.

12) Stephen Ross, "The Harvest Fields: Statistics for 2009," www.wholesomewords.org/missions/greatc.html#birdatrate.

Chapter 1: What Happens When You Die?

1) Ray Pritchard, "Out on a Limb with Shirley MacLaine: Is Reincarnation True?" http://www.keepbelieving.com/sermon/2000-06-04- Out-On-A-Limb-With-Shirley-MacLaine-Is-Reincarnation-True.

2) Colleen Ralson, "Reincarnation," www.watchman.org/na/reincarn. htm.

3) Zachary J. Hayes, "The Purgatorial View," a chapter in the book, *Four Views of Hell*, edited by William Crockett (Grand Rapids, MI: Zondervan Publishing House, 1992), pages 91-118.

4) Timothy George, "Is it unscriptural for a Christian to be cremated?" *Christianity Today* magazine, May 21, 2002.

Chapter 2: What About Resurrection and Judgment?

1) Leslie B. Flynn, *19 Gifts of the Spirit* (David C. Cook Publishers, 1994).

2) A good book about eternal rewards is *Living as if Heaven Matters: Preparing Now for Eternity*, by David Shibley, (Lake Mary, FL: Charisma House, 2007).

Chapter 3: What Will Heaven Be Like?

1) Henry Morris, *The Revelation Record*, (Carol Stream, IL: Tyndale House Publishers, 1983), pages 450-452.

2) The best book in print today about Heaven is one by Randy Alcorn, *Heaven*, (Carol Stream, IL: Tyndale House Publishers, 2004).

3) Alcorn, page 384.

4) Ibid., pages 112, 383.

5) For a detailed discussion of what the Bible says about angels, see "The Ministry of Angels: Past, Present and Future," by Dr. David R. Reagan, *Lamplighter* magazine, July & August 2007, pages 3-8. A copy can be found at www.lamblion.com.

Chapter 4: Is Hell for Real?

1) Conan O'Brien, "I'm Gonna Go to Hell When I Die!" http://www. jesus-is-savior.com/Evils%20in%20America/Hellivision/conan-hell. htm.

2) Sam Lavender, "God Made A Way," http://www.voiceoftheevangelists.com/LinkClick.aspx?fileticket=KUwb1w5pGvU%3D&

tabid=77&mid=431.

3) Ibid.

4) Bon Scott, Angus Young, and Malcolm Young, "Highway to Hell," http://www.metrolyrics.com/highway-to-hell-lyrics-acdc.html.

5) George Carlin, "On Religion," http://www.rense.com/general69/obj. htm.

6) Jonathan Edwards, "The Justice of God in the Damnation of Sinners," http://www.biblebb.com/files/edwards/je-justice.htm.

7) Edward Fudge in a personal email message to the author. Edward Fudge is considered to be one of the foremost theological proponents of the Conditional viewpoint. See his book, *The Fire That Consumes* (Fallbrook, CA: Verdict Publications, 1982). See also "The Conditional View" by Clark H. Pinnock, a chapter in *Four Views on Hell*, edited by William Crockett (Grand Rapids, MI: Zondervan Publishing House, 1992), pages 135-178.

Chapter 5: Are There Many Roads to God?

1) Television interview of Billy Graham by Robert Schuller, May 31, 1997, "On Doctrine," www.ondoctrine.com/10grahab.htm.

2) See, for example, Billy Graham's article, "Why do Christians believe Jesus is the only way of salvation?" (www.billygraham.org/My AnswerArticle.asp?ArticleID=4822). See also, "The Only Way?" (www.billygraham.org/News_Article.asp?ArticleID=354).

3) Graham's consistency in clearly preaching that Jesus is the only way to Heaven is clearly demonstrated in a video clip that can be found on YouTube. The clip, which runs 7 minutes, shows excerpts from 7 sermons delivered between 1957 and the present in which he affirms over and over again that Jesus is the only way to God. The video clip can be found at http://www.youtube.com/watch?v=Vwv 1jiWC4b0. As of March 5, 2010, the video was mislabeled, "Billy Graham denies Jesus . . ." It should be labeled, "Billy Graham affirms Jesus as the only way to God."

4) Two video interviews with Dr. Jeffress have been published as a video album by Lamb & Lion Ministries. The album is titled, "Absolute Truth" and can be ordered at www.lamblion.com or by calling 1-800-705-8316.

5) John Ashbrook, "Billy Graham's Catholic Connection," http://cn view.com/on_line_resources/billy_graham_catholic_connection. htm. This is just one of many examinations on the Internet of Gra-

ham's endorsement of Catholicism. There are also video interviews of him endorsing the Catholic faith.

6) Graham takes this position because he says "Catholics believe in Jesus." But, again, do they simply believe He existed (as do Muslims), or do they believe in the sense of trusting Him, and Him alone, for their salvation? If their trust is truly in Jesus, then why are they instructed to pray to Mary? A great source for unbiblical Catholic beliefs is http://pro-gospel.org/x2.

Chapter 6: How Can We Be Certain Of Life After Death?

1) Much of the material in this chapter concerning the evidence of the Resurrection was gleaned from audio tapes of presentations made by Walter Martin in the 1970's. His daughter, Jill Rische, has made these tapes available on the Internet at www.waltermartin.com.

2) Gary R. Habermas, "Explaining Away Jesus' Resurrection: The Recent Revival of Hallucination Theories," www.garyhabermas.com/articles/crj_explainingaway/crj_explainingaway.htm#ch3.

3) Hugh Schonfield, *The Passover Plot* (New York, NY: Bantam Books, 1965).

4) Blake de Pastino, National Geographic News, "Jesus' Tomb Found in Israel, Filmmakers Claim," February 26, 2007, http://news.nationalgeographic.com/news/2007/02/070226-jesus-tomb.html.

5) LifeSiteNews.com, "Jesus' Family Tomb Discovery is a Titanic Fraud," http://www.lifesitenews.com/ldn/2007/feb/07022601.html.

6) Website of the Lighthouse Free Will Baptist Church in Victoria, Texas can be found at http://www.victorialighthouse.com.

Chapter 7: Are You Living With An Eternal Perspective?

1) Roy Jenkins, *Gladstone: A Biography* (New York, NY: Random House, 1997).

2) There are many versions of this speech that circulate on the Internet, all making the same point. The version reproduced here is a composite prepared by the author.

3) Eugene H. Peterson, *The Message* (Colorado Springs, CO: Navpress Publishing, 2002), page 572.

4) Albert Brumley, "This World is Not My Home (I'm Just A Passing Thru)," a Negro spiritual of unknown origin arranged by Albert E. Brumley. Lyrics can be found at http://arnet.pair.com/RedEllis/lyr/

worldnotmyhome.htm.

5) The author was unable to locate the precise source of this quotation that is attributed to C. S. Lewis. Lewis refers several times to "living on enemy territory" in his classic, *Mere Christianity,* (New York, NY: MacMillan Publishing Co., 1960), p. 51.

6) Tillit S. Teddlie, "Heaven Holds All for Me," public domain. Lyrics and information about the author can be found at http://homeschool blogger.com/hymnstudies/547895.

7) Helen H. Lemmel, "Turn Your Eyes Upon Jesus," © 1922, renewed 1950 by Singspiration, Inc. Lyrics can be found at http://www.cyber hymnal.org/htm/t/u/turnyour.htm. Information about the author can be found at http://www.cyberhymnal.org/bio/l/e/lemmel_hh.htm.

8) You can find the "I am second" video series on the Internet at www. iamsecond.com.

Postscript

1) Ray Pritchard, "At Home with the Lord: What is the Christian View of Death?" July 16, 2003, www.keepbelieving.com.

Songs and Poems

Page 12 – "Leavin' On My Mind," by Rusty Goodman. Lyrics at www. http://sgmidisoundtracks.homestead.com/files/Leaving_On_My_ Mind.htm. Information about Rutsty Goodman can be found at www.sgma.org/inductee_bios/rusty_goodman.htm.

Page 22 – "The Open Door" by Grace Coolidge, www.calvin-coolidge. org/html/poetry.html.

Page 42 – "After the Shadows" by James Rowe. Lyrics at http://ehymn book.org/CMMS/hymnSong.php?folder=p08&id=pd08464. Information about the author can be found at http://www.pdmusic.org/ biographies/Rowe%20James%20Rowe.pdf.

Page 72 – "Heaven" by Randy Estep. Lyrics at www.namethathymn. com/hymn-lyrics-detective-forum/index.php?a=vtopic&t=5623. Nothing could be found about the author.

Page 100 – "Sinners Turn, Why Will Ye Die?" by Charles Wesley. Lyrics at www.ccel.org/w/wesley/hymn/jwg00/jwg0006.html. Biography of the author can be found at http://en.wikipedia.org/wiki/ Charles_Wesley.

Page 118 – "Old Buddha" by Mark Farrow. Lyrics at http://unwilted. blogspot.com/2004/06/oh-buddha.html. No information could be found about the author.

Page 136 – "Up From the Grave" by Robert Lowry. Lyrics at http:// www.cyberhymnal.org/htm/l/i/lintgrav.htm. Information about the author can be found at http://en.wikipedia.org/wiki/Robert_ Lowry _(hymn_writer).

Page 158 – "Ozymandias" by Percy Bysshe Shelley, http://en.wiki pedia.org/wiki/Percy_Bysshe_Shelley.

Page 182 – "Thanantopsis" by William Cullen Bryant. The poem can be found at http://www.bartleby.com/102/16.html. Information about Bryant can be found at http://en.wikipedia.org/wiki/William _Cullen_Bryant.

Page 186 – "God of the Living" by John Ellerton. Lyrics at http://www. cyberhymnal.org/htm/g/l/gliweyes.htm. Information about Ellerton can be found at http://www.hymnary.org/person/Ellerton_J.

A Traditional Child's Prayer

Now I lay me down to sleep,
I pray the Lord my soul to keep.
If I should die before I wake,
I pray the Lord my soul to take.

The Author and His Ministry

About the Author

Dr. David R. Reagan is the senior evangelist for Lamb & Lion Ministries. He is a native Texan who resides in Allen, Texas, a suburb of Dallas. He is married and is the father of two daughters. His wife, Ann, is a retired first grade teacher. They have four grandchildren and two great grandchildren.

Dr. Reagan is a Phi Beta Kappa graduate of the University of Texas in Austin. Upon graduation from the university, he was awarded a Woodrow Wilson Fellowship which he used to attend graduate school. His graduate degrees were earned in the field of International Law and Politics from the Fletcher School of Law & Diplomacy, a graduate school of international relations owned and operated jointly by Tufts and Harvard Universities.

Before entering the ministry in 1980, Dr. Reagan had an extensive career in higher education which included the following positions: Assistant to the President of Austin College in Sherman, Texas; President of South Texas Jr. College in Houston; Director of Pepperdine University's Center for International Business in Los Angeles; and Vice President of Phillips University in Enid, Oklahoma.

In the mid-60's Dr. Reagan served as a Fulbright Lecturer at the University of the Philippines and toured all of Southeast Asia lecturing on U.S. foreign policy.

Dr. Reagan is a life-long Bible student, teacher, and preacher. He is the author of many religious essays which have been published in a wide variety of journals and magazines. He has written eight books and numerous booklets, and he serves as the editor of the ministry's bi-monthly *Lamplighter* magazine. Audio and video versions of his sermons have been distributed world wide. His books have been translated into several languages.

Invitations have come from all over the world for Dr. Reagan to speak. He has conducted prophecy conferences in Russia, Poland, Hungary, Austria, the Czech Republic, Belarus, Israel, South Africa, India, China, Mexico, the Philippines, and England (including Wales, Scotland, and Northern Ireland). He has led more than forty pilgrimages to Israel that focus on the prophetic significance of the sites visited.

For 22 years Dr. Reagan was the spokesman on Lamb & Lion's daily radio program called "Christ in Prophecy," which was broadcast nationally.

In September 2002, the radio program was converted into a weekly television program that is broadcast nationally over the Daystar Television Network, the Inspiration Network, the National Religious Broadcaster's Network, and The Church Channel. These networks provide access to over 70 million homes in the United States, and through Daystar's international satellite system, the program has access to every country in the world.

Dr. Reagan's television program, "Christ in Prophecy," deals with the prophetic significance of national and international events, showing how they relate to end time prophecies about the return of Jesus.

Dr. Reagan is also the featured speaker on many video programs produced by Lamb & Lion Ministries, including several that have been videotaped in Israel. His video album titled, *The Fundamentals of Bible Prophecy*, contains six programs that provide an overview of the nature and meaning of Bible prophecy. He has also written and produced several multi-media Bible prophecy teaching kits.

About the Ministry

Lamb & Lion Ministries was founded in 1980 as a non-denominational, independent ministry. The Ministry does not seek to convert people to any particular church. Rather, it seeks to lift up Jesus and draw people to Him as Lord and Savior.

The Ministry was established for the purpose of proclaiming the soon return of Jesus. The Ministry believes that although it is not possible to know the date when Jesus will return, it is possible to know the season of His return, and that we are in that season now.

The message of the Ministry is directed at both believers and non-believers. To the unsaved, the Ministry says, "Flee from the wrath that is to come by fleeing into the loving arms of Jesus." To believers, the Ministry says, "Commit yourselves to holiness and evangelism as you await the appearance of your Blessed Hope." The Ministry believes that Jesus is the only hope for the world today. He is the Gospel — the "Good News."

The Ministry believes the Church, as expressed through the local congregation, is the basic unit of God's plan for the proclamation of the Gospel and the discipling of believers. Lamb & Lion Ministries exists to serve the Church in its effort to win souls for Christ and to disciple those who accept the Lord.

Over the years, Lamb & Lion Ministries has been instrumental in helping establish five other Bible prophecy ministries, four here in the United States and one in Northern Ireland.

Dr. Reagan's Comprehensive Book About Bible Prophecy

What is the destiny of planet earth?

What is going to be the fate of mankind?

We don't have to guess. The Bible spells out God's plan for the ages in great detail through prophecies given thousands of years ago.

In this book Dr. Reagan presents a panoramic survey of the fundamentals of Bible prophecy, with a focus on the prophecies that relate to the end times. In the process, he reveals God's plan for the redemption of mankind and the restoration of the creation.

The book is written in a down-to-earth, easy-to-understand style. Although all the chapters relate to the overall theme, each chapter is designed to stand alone. This makes it possible for you either to read the book straight through or to skip around, reading only those chapters whose topics appeal to you.

The book is divided into five parts:

> Prophetic Significance
> Prophetic Issues
> Prophetic Viewpoints
> Prophetic Signs
> Prophetic Hope

There is a Prophetic Epilogue in which Dr. Reagan presents an in-depth, verse by verse explanation of Psalm 2, one of the Bible's greatest passages about the Second Coming of the Lord.

The book contains 42 chapters and runs 415 pages in length. It sells for $15. You can order a copy by calling 800-705-8316, Monday through Friday, 8am to 5pm Central time. You can also purchase the book through the Lamb & Lion website at www.lamblion.com.

Dr. Reagan's Video Overview of Bible Prophecy

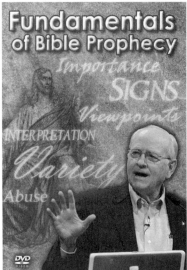

This album contains six programs on two DVDs. Each program runs about 25 minutes in length, for a total of 150 minutes. The album loads with a menu that enables the viewer to jump immediately to any one of the six programs.

All six lessons were presented by Dr. David Reagan before live audiences. They provide a comprehensive introduction to all the fundamentals of Bible prophecy:

- The Abuse of Bible Prophecy
- The Importance of Bible Prophecy
- The Variety of Bible Prophecy
- The Interpretation of Bible Prophecy
- The End Time Viewpoints
- The Signs of the Times

One of the DVD discs contains printable files for a Teacher's Manual and Student Study Guides.

This album is a great resource for both learning and teaching Bible prophecy. Each presentation is lavishly illustrated with pictures, charts, and diagrams. The album sells for $25.

You can order a copy by calling 800-705-8316, Monday through Friday, 8am to 5pm Central time. You can also purchase the book through the Lamb & Lion website at www.lamblion.com.

The Lamb & Lion Website

The Lamb & Lion website is an interactive site that you can use to pose questions to the ministry's Web Minister. The site also contains a host of articles about every aspect of Bible prophecy. Additionally, you can view the ministry's television programs on the site and read copies of the ministry's magazine. The ministry's catalogue of Bible prophecy resources can also be found on the website, and orders can be placed from the site.